Sock Anatomy

Dissecting Socks: Heels and Toes

Second Version

Second Edition

May 2017

Layout Design: Clare Devine

Technical Editing: Jo Kelly

Copy Editing: Jo Milmine

Model: Jessica James

Sample Knitting: Michelle Hazel, Jessica James and Cath Thorley

For Maeve
'my first sock muse'

Contents

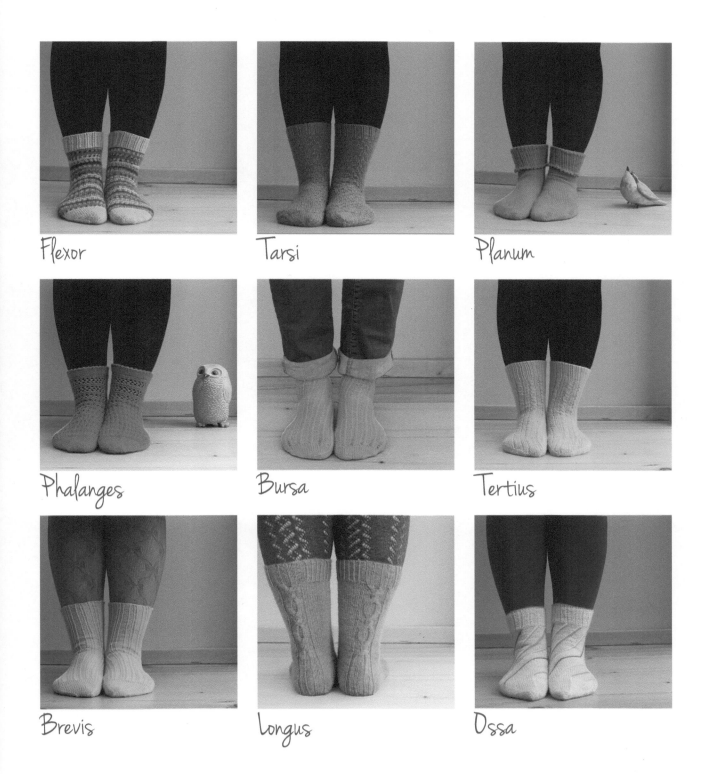

Flexor

Tarsi

Planum

Phalanges

Bursa

Tertius

Brevis

Longus

Ossa

Introduction

When I started knitting I always swore I would never ever knit socks. You know what they say about "never say never"... I am now well and truly hooked on sock knitting.

This book was born from the idea of trying the many different ways of turning a heel without committing to a full size adult sock. Often a new technique is best learnt and practised on a small scale, before we unleash our knitting powers on a larger, more complicated pattern. Baby socks are the perfect vehicle for trying things out. They are quick and easy, take minimal yarn and result in the cutest itty-bitty socks.

Since I launched Sock Anatomy, I have met so many inspiring knitters and my sock knitting journey has taken me on lots of exciting adventures. One of the recurring themes when I speak to people was the desire to have these cute itty-bitty socks in a wider range of sizes.

After all, we all want to take the skills we learn and extend them. I have revised all of the patterns in this book to include a full range of sizes.

The information sections have also been updated and additional content has been included to help you on your sock knitting journey.

Thanks
Clare

Getting started

Selecting Materials

Choosing the right tools for the job is important when knitting socks. It will really help you to enjoy the knitting process and turn out beautiful and useful finished items. This section aims to give you a general overview of how I select my sock knitting materials. Remember though, knitting is about personal choices and using what works for you. This section is only intended as a guide; you may find different solutions that suit you better.

Yarn

When choosing sock yarn I would recommend selecting a blend with a high wool content. The natural fibres are important in creating a good fabric that results in a well-fitted sock. Additionally, natural fibres have the excellent wicking properties needed for socks.

Many sock yarns contain a percentage of nylon or other synthetic fibre. This reinforces the yarn, giving it the robust qualities needed to face up to the task of clothing our feet day in and day out. Babies are not very hard on their socks, so you might want to try some of the softer blends too. Always think about how the yarn is going to combine with the stitch pattern when selecting your materials.

There are many wonderful sock yarns on the market today, with options to suit all budgets and a beautiful range of colours. Whether you choose a commercial yarn or some exquisitely crafted hand dyed yarn, here are my top tips to help you make the best choice for your current project.

Top Tips for Choosing Sock Yarn

1) Look for something with a high twist. This is what gives the yarn the structure you need for longer wearing socks.

2) Nylon is a helpful addition to look for. You can either choose a yarn that is blended with nylon or add nylon as a reinforcement material in the heels and toes.

3) Although helpful, nylon isn't always required, as there are many natural fibre blends which have hard-wearing properties that will create great socks. You can read more about using different blends in an interview with Sue Blacker on my website.

4) Think about the colour and texture of the yarn in relation to your pattern. For example, a highly variegated yarn will make it difficult to see delicate details in a pattern, and yarns with a halo can obscure pattern features. Conversely, a lighter coloured yarn will help your cables to pop.

5) Experiment with as many yarns as you can. The more you try, the better equipped you will be to know what works for you. Most importantly, knit with what you love!
Needles

Knitting in the Round

To knit socks you need to be able to knit in the round with your chosen needles. While I prefer to knit in the round using magic loop for socks, you can knit these patterns using any method you are comfortable with. Please bear in mind, the patterns are written for magic loop and therefore assume you will have your stitches divided equally over two needles for the vast majority of knitting time. I have used markers to indicate where increases and decreases or short rows should take place. This will make it easier to transfer instructions to DPNs.

I would always recommend starting with the method you already use for knitting in the round, or the one that most appeals to you if you have never knitted in the round before. You can knit socks using Double Pointed Needles (using four or five needles), magic loop (using a long circular needle), on two circular needles or with a small circular needle (usually measuring 23cm / 9").

It is important to experiment; remember there is no right or wrong needle set-up for sock knitting. It depends on what is easiest for you, and which best matches the pattern you are working on.

Which Needles Should I Use?

Choosing needles is a matter of personal preference. I have had love affairs with many needles over the years and use different brands or types depending on the project and yarn. There are a few things I think you need to consider when selecting your needles for a sock project.

Wooden or Metal?

Think about how the needle will interact with the fibre. Wood tends to grip the yarn a little more than metal needles. This can help with slippery yarn and is especially useful with silk-based yarns. As with all needles each brand will be slightly different and some of the wood finishes can be smoother than others.

Metal needles are my favourite, although some people find metal can be cold on the hands. As with wooden needles the finish on the surface can really alter your knitting experience. Some needles have a brushed finish that provides added grip; others are very smooth and sleek.

Each needle has its merits and will serve different purposes appealing to different styles of knitting. Choosing needles is very much a matter of trial and error. I would urge you try as many needles as you can. Ask others what they think and definitely try one pair of needles before investing in a whole set.

The Value of Sharp Points

I prefer a nice sharp point on my needles. I find it is perfect for little stitches and intricate patterns. You might find a sharp point splits your yarn. Again, it is trial and error. Work with the needle that best suits your knitting style and the kind of yarn you are using for the project.

Magic Loop and the Quality of your Cable

Something I think is absolutely crucial when knitting socks using magic loop is your cable. I always check the cable when picking up a set of knitting needles. Is it going to bend with me or fight against me as I try to execute that wonderful loop for knitting socks? If your cable is stiff, you run the real risk of creating unsightly ladders up the sides of your sock. You want something that is smooth and flexible that will make knitting in the round with magic loop a joy and not a trial. Equally important is the join between the cable and the needle. This must be smooth, as a rough edge and gaps at the join will mean your yarn frequently gets stuck. This is bound to detract from the pleasure you should derive from knitting socks.

Extras

The two main accessories I think you need for sock knitting are stitch markers and a tapestry needle.

The needle is for weaving in ends and any tapestry needle will do.

The stitch markers are helpful for all sorts of things. I find locking stitch markers the most useful. Using this style of stitch marker means you can attach it to your knitting instead of having it on the needles, where it inevitably ends up scooting up and down the cable of your magic loop, or falling off the end of the needle.

I also try to have at least two colours on hand. This allows me to mark different portions of the sock and I find it makes learning a new technique that much easier. If you only have one colour you could always attach another small stitch marker to the lockable loop or tie a scrap of waste yarn to differentiate between the marker placements. In some places you may have four markers on the go at once and being able to quickly tell them apart will really make life easier.

Sock Construction

Top down or toe up? There are many arguments about which is the best method of knitting and some knitters swear by either top down or toe up. They certainly offer slightly different fit and style options. To dispel a knitting myth I often hear, you can certainly try on socks as you go regardless of the direction you are knitting.

Each direction poses its challenges. Toe up cast on methods can prove a little tricky and for top down many people find Kitchener Stitch a little challenging at first. That said, all of these techniques are easy to master with a time and practice.

I would urge you to try both methods and see what suits your knitting style and personal preferences. Experimentation is the key!

Heels

There are many different ways to create a sock heel. This book covers three main themes and some key variations on those themes: heel flaps, short row heels and afterthought heels. The next few pages contain diagrams that show you the key elements of the various heels and sock constructions.

Toes

As with heels, there are many ways to finish the toes. This book has a variety of options for shaping the toe. Choosing the toe depends on a few things, the main ones being fit and style or aesthetic. You can find more information on toes on my website.

Afterthought Heel
from the top down or toe up

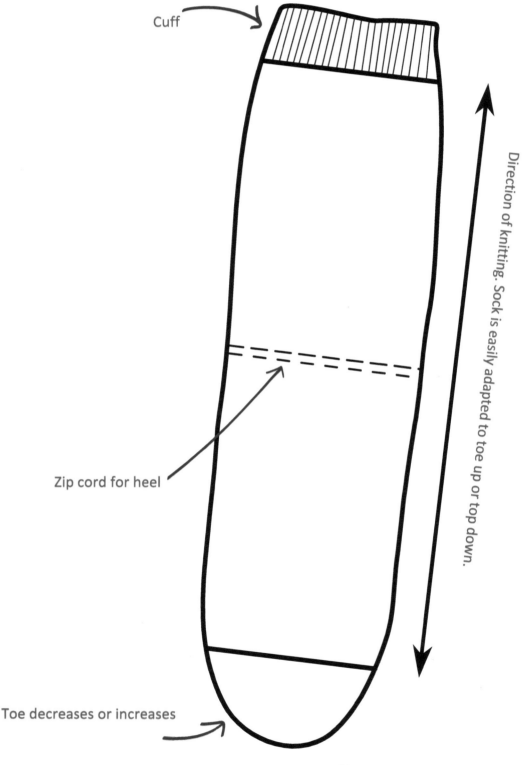

Cuff

Zip cord for heel

Direction of knitting. Sock is easily adapted to toe up or top down.

Toe decreases or increases

The afterthought heel sock is created in two stages. First, you create the foot and leg, essentially knitting a tube sock.

Then you pick up stitches for the heel and create a heel cup.

This is a perfect sock for beginner sock knitters.

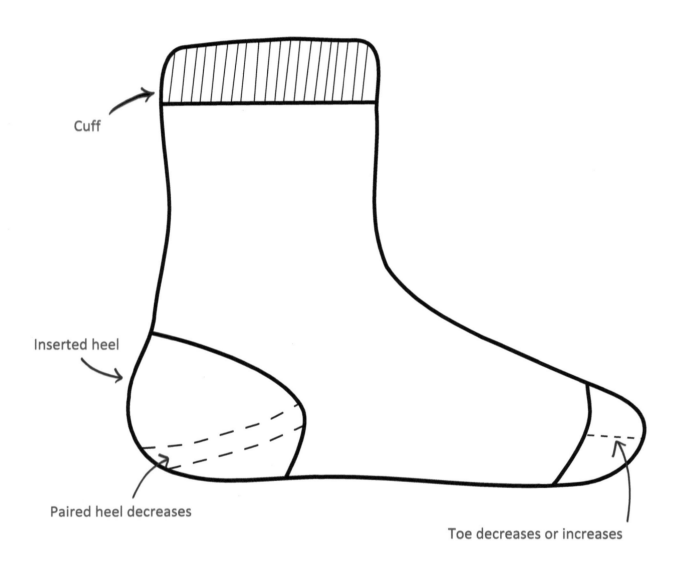

Cuff

Inserted heel

Paired heel decreases

Toe decreases or increases

Heel Flap *from the top down*

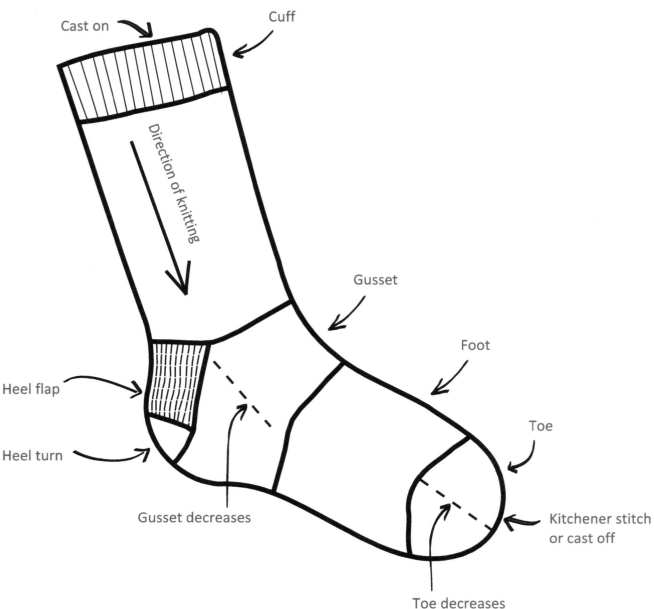

Cast on

Cuff

Direction of knitting

Gusset

Foot

Heel flap

Heel turn

Toe

Gusset decreases

Kitchener stitch or cast off

Toe decreases

The heel flap is created in three main steps. The heel flap itself is knitted back and forth, the heel is then turned using short rows and the stitches along the side of the heel flap picked up to join the sock in the round again. The last step is the gusset where a set of paired decreases is worked to bring the total number of stitches back to the correct number needed for the foot.

This book has four different heel methods for you to try.

Heel Flap from the toe up

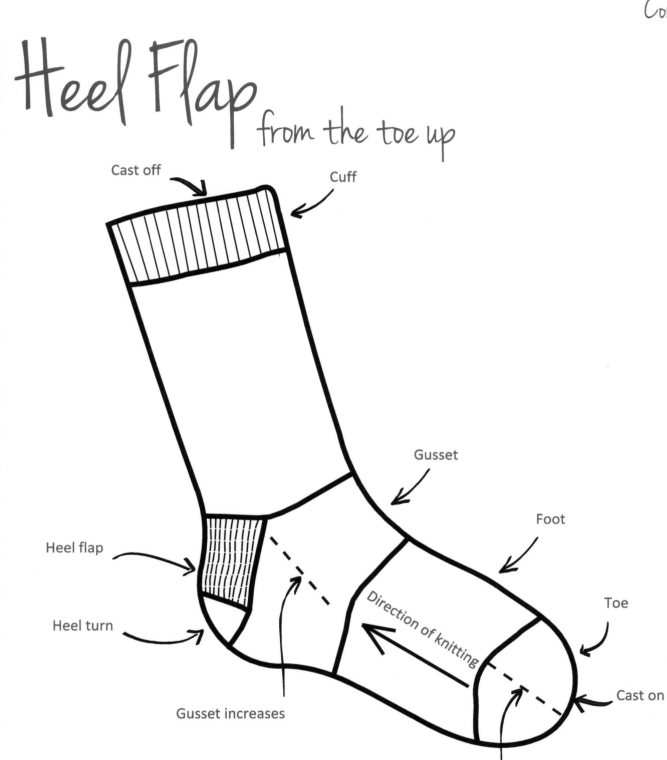

Cast off

Cuff

Gusset

Foot

Heel flap

Toe

Heel turn

Direction of knitting

Cast on

Gusset increases

Toe increases

The heel flap from the toe up is slightly different from its top down cousin. The gusset is worked using paired increases and then the heel is turned using short rows. Once this has taken place a faux heel flap is created working back and forth, while being joined to the body of the sock using decreases.

This style of heel is well suited to those with a high instep.

Short Row Heel
from the top down

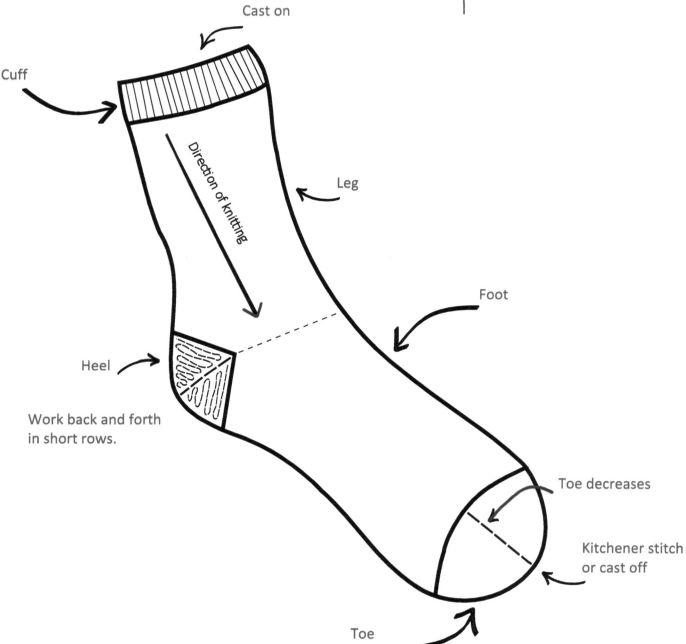

Cast on

Cuff

Direction of Knitting

Leg

Foot

Heel

Work back and forth
in short rows.

Toe decreases

Kitchener stitch
or cast off

Toe

The short row heel is created using a series of short rows, and is worked in the same way for both the top down and toe up versions. The short rows are created with wraps and turns, giving a neat finish to your completed sock.

The short row heel can be worked in either stocking stitch or garter stitch. Both examples are featured in this book.

15

Short Row Heel
from the toe up

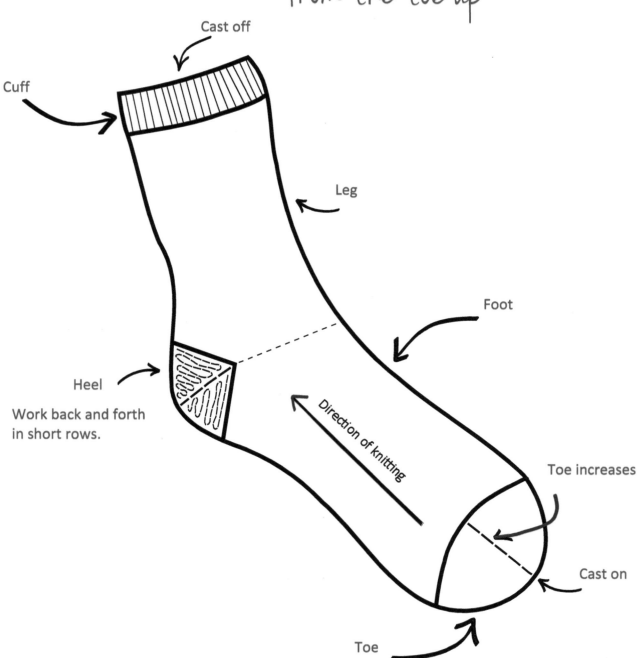

Cast off

Cuff

Leg

Foot

Heel

Work back and forth
in short rows.

Direction of knitting

Toe increases

Cast on

Toe

If you have not worked with short rows before, there is a step by step guide included on page 18 of this booklet.

Techniques

There are some general sock knitting techniques you will find making a regular appearance in my patterns. To make sure you always have access to the latest content, I have included a tutorials and techniques section on my website.

www.yarnandpointysticks.com

Casting On

Getting a flexible edge for top down socks is vital. I always recommend using stretchy cast on, such as the Long Tail Cast On, or my personal favourite, the German Twisted Cast On.

Toe up socks need a beautiful, seamless start in life and while there are a few different ways of getting started, I highly recommend Judy Becker's Magic Cast On.

Casting Off and Finishing

Top down socks need a seamless finish; I would always caution against anything but grafting for your toes. The Kitchener stitch was devised to close socks with a comfortable seamless finish. It requires a little bit of concentration but is well worth the effort. A detailed photo tutorial can be found on page 19.

Toe up socks need a firm but stretchy cast off. I love Elizabeth Zimmerman's Sewn Bind off to finish my toe up socks. If you prefer something with more stretch, you might like to try Jeny's Surprisingly Stretchy Bind Off.

Short Rows

There are many different methods for creating short rows. The most common is the wrap and turn method: written instructions are given on the next page and a detailed photo tutorial can be found on my website. If you do not enjoy this method you could consider one of the other techniques including Japanese Short Rows (wrapless short rows), German Short Rows (yarn over short rows) and shadow wraps.

The tutorial pages on my website contain an up to date list of resources.

Short rows

There are two ways to work the Wrap and Turn (W&T) needed for short rows. This is my preferred method when knitting socks.

Right side / knit rows

Step 1: Slip stitch to be wrapped from LH needle to RH needle, purlwise, with yarn in back
Step 2: Bring yarn to the front, around the stitch to be wrapped
Step 3: Slip stitch to be wrapped from RH needle to LH needle, without twisting
Step 4: Turn work and bring yarn through to the front (between last worked stitch and wrapped stitch) ready to work a purl row.

Wrong side / purl rows

Step 1: Slip stitch to be wrapped from LH needle to RH needle, purlwise, with yarn in front
Step 2: Bring yarn to the back, around the stitch to be wrapped
Step 3: Slip stitch to be wrapped from RH needle to LH needle, without twisting
Step 4: Turn work and take yarn through to the back (between last worked stitch and wrapped stitch) ready to work a knit row.

When you work back across you need to work the wraps in with your stitches to create a neat finish. The method differs slightly depending on whether you are working on the RS or the WS.

Right side / knit rows

Step 1: Pick up the wrap from front to back
Step 2: Insert the RH needle into the wrapped stitch
Step 3: Knit the wrapped stitch and the wrap together

Wrong side / purl rows

Step 1: Pick up the wrap from back to front
Step 2: Place the wrap onto the LH needle
Step 3: Purl the wrapped stitch and the wrap together

Kitchener stitch

Set up row - complete steps one to three, once.

Step 1: Divide your stitches evenly across the needles and hold as shown
Step 2: Bring tapestry needle through **front** stitch as if to **purl**, leave the stitch on the needle
Step 3: Bring tapestry needle through **back** stitch as if to **knit**, leave the stitch on the needle

Repeat steps 4 to 9 until all stitches have been worked

Step 4: Bring tapestry needle through **front** stitch as if to **knit**
Step 5: Slip the stitch worked in step four **off the needle**
Step 6: Bring tapestry needle through **front** stitch as if to **purl**, leave the stitch **on the needle**

Step 7: Bring tapestry needle through **back** stitch as if to **purl**
Step 8: Slip the stitch worked in step eight **off the needle**
Step 9: Bring tapestry needle through **back** stitch as if to **knit**, leave the stitch **on the needle**

Repeat steps 4 to 9 until all stitches have been worked.

I find repeating this in my head as I complete the kitchener stitch really helpful.

Front, knit off, purl on, back, purl off, knit on
Front, knit off, purl on, back, purl off, knit on

Sizing

Babies, toddlers and younger children

Foot sizes vary; it is recommended you knit the socks to suit the measurements of the recipient's foot. If you can't measure their foot, I have included a size guide by age. When knitting for young babies, I always recommend making the sock slightly larger than you think it needs to be, as babies grow very quickly and they don't need super fitted socks. If you are knitting for toddlers who are wearing shoes, the socks will need to be a little more fitted.

Suggested age / measurements

Size	unstretched circ	recommended to fit	Suggested foot length
0-6 months	11.5cm / 4.5"	12.5 - 14cm / 5 – 5.5"	8.5 – 10cm / 3.25 – 4"
6-12 month	13cm / 5"	14 - 15cm / 5.5 - 6"	10 – 11.5cm / 4 – 4.5"
Toddler	14cm / 5.5"	15 - 16cm / 6 – 6.25"	11.5 – 13cm / 4.5 – 5"
Child	15cm / 6"	16 - 17cm / 6.25 - 7"	13 – 14.5cm / 5 – 5.75"

Knitting for older children who are wearing shoes

Some people prefer not to have a patterned foot, as they feel the texture can make the foot uncomfortable in the shoe. You can always choose the leave the pattern off the foot and knit in plain stocking stitch (knit each round) if you think this will be more comfortable. You are able to do this on all the socks, however some designs will lend themselves to this modification better than others.

Older children and adult sizes

All patterns have five adult sizes.

The smaller sizes would also be suitable for older children too. It is vital that you measure the foot of the recipient. Remember that socks should be knitted with negative ease, meaning the finished circumference of the sock is less than the actual measurement of the foot. I usually recommend about 2.5cm / 1" of negative ease for adult socks. For more information refer to the tutorial pages on my website www.yarnandpointysticks.com

Some patterns have more elasticity than others and need a little more negative ease to create a good fit. This is particularly noticeable in the lace socks like Bursa and Phalanges.

Size	unstretched circumference	recommended to fit
XS	16cm / 6.5"	18cm / 7.25"
S	17.5cm / 7"	19.5cm / 7.5"
M	20cm / 8"	22cm / 8.5"
L	22.5cm / 9"	24.5cm / 9.5"
XL	25cm / 10"	27cm / 10.5"

Each sock has its own unique fit properties and this needs to be taken into account when choosing which pattern is most suitable for your needs. Please remember that some heels are more suitable that others for certain foot shapes. If there are particular constraints of a specific style details will be noted in the pattern notes.

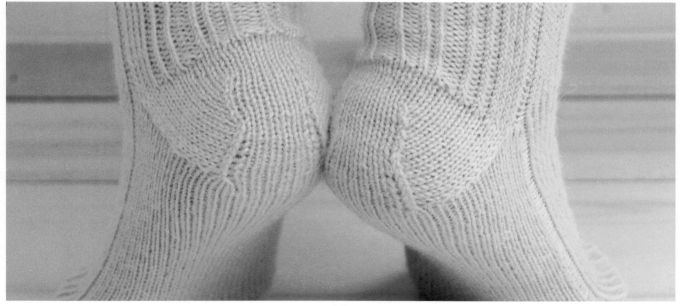

About the Designs

This collection contains nine patterns each focusing on different heels and toes.

Flexor

This easy knit is ideal as an introduction to sock knitting and great for knitting on the go. These afterthought heel socks can be knitted from the top down or the toe up, making them perfect for experimenting with direction. Choose your favourite self-patterning yarn, paired with contrast heels and toes for happy feet.

Tarsi

The perfect balance of texture and rhythmic knitting combine harmoniously in Tarsi. Knitted from the top down, with a traditional heel flap construction and rounded heel turn, this is a great universal sock pattern. The textured stitch works equally well with solids, semi-solids and variegated yarn, each producing its own unique take on the Tarsi texture.

Planum

Fabulous toe up socks for everyone: Planum is the ideal choice for all the family. The faux heel flap offers a great fit, especially for those with high insteps, and the clever fold-over ribbed cuff is designed to stay up while looking stylish. Add a feminine finish with a picot edge, or leave the ribbed cuff plain for a practical, unisex look.

Phalanges

Sometimes we need a touch of lace to clothe our dancing feet. These pretty lace socks feature simple lace panels framed by garter ridges. Knitted from the toe up, this sock has a short row heel and a folded picot hemmed cuff.

Bursa

Fun ankle socks, perfect for warmer weather. Columns of eyelets and garter stitch create a lovely textured openwork fabric. This sock is knitted from the top down and features a soft and squishy garter stitch short row heel.

Tertius

Everybody needs a pair of cabled socks! These socks feature columns of mini cables that are a great introduction to cable knitting. Knitted from the top down, these socks feature a ribbed heel flap and a V or half-handkerchief heel turn.

Brevis

Nothing hugs your feet quite like a pair of ribbed socks. Brevis uses twisted ribbing to give this simple sock a beautifully structured look. The heel is constructed with a heel flap and turned using a German or band heel turn. Unisex socks for the whole family.

Longus

Make a statement with the elongated cable of Longus taking centre stage. Knitted from the top down, these socks are slightly longer than the others. They feature a decorative heel flap and the heel is turned using a Dutch or square heel.

Ossa

Swirls of colour dance and play around Ossa: the perfect blank canvas for using up sock scraps. This sock is knitted from the top down and features an afterthought heel. The heel and toe are shaped using swirl decreases, which often look a little unusual but fit beautifully.

Abbreviations

BOR	beginning of round
CO	cast on
CC	contrast colour
K	knit
KCC	knit using the contrast colour yarn
Ktbl	knit through the back loop
K2tog	knit two stitches together
K3tog	knit three stitches together
LH needle	left hand needle
LT	left twist (see step by step photo tutorial for this at the end of the pattern)
M(A)	marker / letter in () denotes which marker
M1	make one: lift bar from the back of knitting and knit through the front of the stitch
M1R	make one right: lift bar from the back of knitting and knit through the front of the stitch
M1L	make one left: lift bar from the front of knitting and knit through the back of the stitch
MC	main colour
P2tog	purl two stitches together
PM	place marker
P	purl
PU	pick up
Rnd	round
Rpt	repeat
RM	remove marker
RS	right side
Sl1	slip one stitch purlwise with yarn in back
Skpo	slip one stitch as if to knit, k1, pass slipped stitch over knitted stitch
SSK	slip two stitches, one at a time as if to knit, onto the RH needle; insert tip of LH needle into front of two stitches and knit them together
SSSK	slip three stitches, one at a time as if to knit, onto the RH needle; insert tip of LH needle into front of three stitches and knit them together
SM	slip marker
WS	wrong side
W&T	wrap and turn
YO	yarn over
2/1 LC	slip two stitches onto a cable needle and hold in front; k1, k2 from cable needle
1/3 LPC	slip three stitches onto a cable needle and hold in front; purl one stitch, then knit three stitches from cable needle
1/3 RPC	slip one stitch onto a cable needle and hold in back; knit next three stitches, then purl the stitch from the cable needle
3/3 RC	slip three stitches onto a cable needle and hold in back; knit three stitches, then knit three stitches from cable needle

Patterns

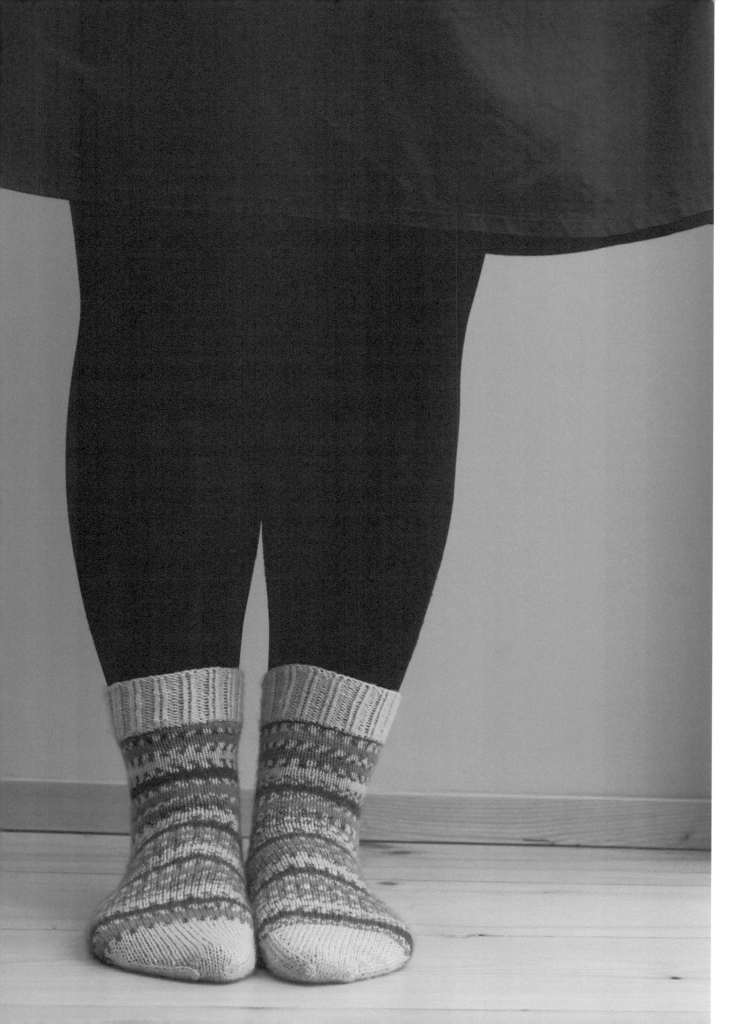

This easy knit is ideal as an introduction to sock knitting and great for knitting on the go. These afterthought heel socks can be knitted from the top down or the toe up, perfect for experimenting with direction. Choose your favourite self-patterning yarn, paired with contrast heels and toes for happy dancing feet.

Materials

West Yorkshire Spinners Signature (4 ply; 75% wool, 25% nylon; 400m/437 yds per 100g ball)
MC Shade: Blue Tit; 1 x 100g ball
CC Shade: Butterscotch; 1 x 100g ball

Yardage per size varies. Baby and toddler (allow 30g MC and 10g CC), child (allow 40g MC and 10g CC), adult sizes will depend on the size and foot length; allow up to 100g MC and up to 40g CC depending on size. It is unlikely that you will need more than 100g of MC unless you are knitting for very large feet.

2.5mm / US 1.5 needle for working in the round
Four stitch markers
Tapestry needle

Gauge

32 sts and 44 rows to 10cm / 4" in stocking stitch worked in the round, blocked.

Sizes

0-6m (6-12m, toddler, child) [XS, S, M, L, XL]

Finished circumference (unstretched): 11.5 (13, 14, 15) [16, 17.5, 20, 22.5, 25] cm / 4.5 (5, 5.5, 6) [6.5, 7, 8, 9, 10]"

To fit approx: 12.5 - 14 (14 - 15, 15 - 16, 16 - 17) [18, 19.5, 22, 24,5, 27] cm / 5 – 5.5 (5.5 - 6, 6 - 6.25, 6.25 - 7) [7.25, 7.5, 8.5, 9.5, 10.5]"

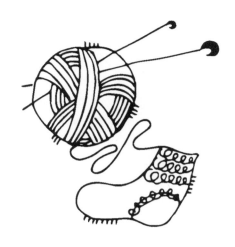

Pattern notes

The pattern gives you options for knitting top down or toe up, meaning you can choose the method you are most comfortable with, or try a new way of knitting socks.

Pattern

Top down

Using CC; CO 36 (40, 44, 48) [52, 56, 64, 72, 80], PM for start of round and join knitting for working in the round, being careful not to twist.

Cuff

The cuff is worked in 2x2 twisted rib.

Rnd 1: *k2 tbl, p2; repeat from * to end of rnd.
Repeat this rnd until cuff measures 2 (2, 3, 3) [4, 4, 5, 5, 5) cm / 0.75 (0.75, 1.25, 1.25) [1.5, 1.5, 2, 2, 2]" or desired length.

Leg

Next rnd: knit.

Change to MC.

Knit for 3 (4, 5, 6) [8, 8, 10, 10, 10) cm / 1.25 (1.5, 2, 2.5) [3.25, 3.25, 4, 4, 4]" or desired length.

Place waste yarn for heel.

Using waste yarn, k18 (20, 22, 24) [26, 28, 32, 36, 40] sts.
Return these sts from RH needle to LH needle.
Using MC knit one rnd.

Foot

When working the foot, you need to take into account that the heel and toe will add length when they are knitted.

Knit until distance from waste yarn for heel is 6 (7, 7, 8) [8, 9, 10, 12, 13] cm / 2.5 (2.75, 2.75, 3.25) [3.25, 3.5, 4, 4.75, 5.25]" less than is required for the foot.

Next rnd: k18 (20, 22, 24) [26, 28, 32, 36, 40] PM, k to end of rnd.

Toe

Change to CC.

Rnd 1: *k1, ssk, knit to 3 sts before M, k2tog, k1; rpt from * to end of rnd.
Rnd 2: knit.

Repeat these two rnds 5 (6, 6, 7) [8, 9, 10, 12, 13] more times.
12 (12, 16, 16) [16, 16, 20, 20, 24) sts rem.

Use Kitchener stitch to graft the toe closed.

Toe up

Using CC and Judy's Magic Cast on, CO 12 (12, 16, 16) [16, 16, 20, 20, 24] sts, PM for start of round.

Toe

Rnd 1: k6 (6, 8, 8) [8, 8, 10, 10, 12], PM, k6tbl (k6tbl, k8tbl, k8tbl) [k8tbl, k8tbl, k10tbl, k10tbl, k12tbl].
Rnd 1: *k1, M1R, knit to last st before M, M1L, k1; rpt from * to end of rnd.
Rnd 2: knit.

Repeat these two rnds 5 (6, 6, 7) [8, 9, 10, 12, 13] more times. 36 (40, 44, 48) [52, 56, 64, 72, 80] sts.

Foot

Change to MC.

Knit until foot measures 3 (3.5, 3.5, 4) [4.5, 5, 5.5, 6.5, 7] cm / 1.25 (1.5, 1.5, 1.5) [1.75, 2, 2.25, 2.5, 2.75]" less than desired finished length.

Place waste yarn for heel.

Using waste yarn; k18 (20, 22, 24) [26, 28, 32, 36, 40] sts.
Return these sts from RH needle to LH needle.
Knit one rnd.

Leg

Knit for 3 (4, 5, 6) [8, 8, 10, 10, 10] cm / 1 (1.5, 2, 2.5) [3.25, 3.25, 4, 4, 4]" or desired length.

Cuff

Change to CC

The cuff is worked in 2x2 twisted rib.

Rnd 1: knit.
Rnd 2: *k2 tbl, p2; repeat from * to end of rnd.
Repeat this rnd until cuff measures 2 (2, 3, 3) [4, 4, 5, 5, 5) cm / 0.75 (0.75, 1.23, 1.25) [1.5, 1.5, 2, 2, 2]" or desired length.

Bind off using a stretchy bind off, such as the Elizabeth Zimmerman Sewn Bind Off.

Heel

The heel is knitted in the same way for both the toe up and top down version.

Carefully unravel the waste yarn, placing the stitches on your needles as you go.

Check you have an equal number of sts on each needle: 36 (40, 44, 48) [52, 56, 64, 72, 80] total sts / 18 (20, 22, 24) [26, 28, 32, 36, 40] sts on each needle.

To avoid holes at either side of the heel you need to pick up two extra stitches when you get to the gap between the top and bottom needle on each side, picking up a total of four sts this round. You will decrease these on the next round. You also need to place a marker to note where you will decrease for the heel.

Using CC

Rnd 1: M1 k18 (20, 22, 24) [26, 28, 32, 36, 40], M1, PM, M1, k18 (20, 22, 24) [26, 28, 32, 36, 40], M1.

40 (44, 48, 52) [56, 60, 68, 76, 84] sts.

Rnd 2: *k1, ssk, knit to 3 sts before M, k2tog, k1; rpt from * to end of rnd.

Rnd 3: knit.
Rnd 4: *k1, ssk, knit to 3 sts before M, k2tog, k1; rpt from * to end of rnd.

Repeat these last two rnds 5 (6, 6, 7) [8, 9, 10, 12, 13] more times.

12 (12, 16, 16) [16, 16, 20, 20, 24] sts rem.

Use Kitchener stitch to graft the heel closed.

The perfect balance of texture and rhythmic knitting combine harmoniously in Tarsi. Knitted from the top down, with a traditional heel flap construction and rounded heel turn, these are a great universal sock pattern. The textured stitch works equally well with solids, semi-solids and variegated yarn, each producing its own unique take on the Tarsi texture.

Materials

West Yorkshire Spinners Signature (4 ply; 75% wool, 25% nylon; 400m/437 yds per 100g ball)
Shade: Cardamom; 1 x 100g ball

Yardage per size varies. Baby and toddler (allow 35 – 40g), child (allow 50 – 60g), adult sizes will depend on the size and foot length; allow up to 100g for XS, S and M in a UK size 6. For larger sizes and over a UK size 7 you may need up to 150g of yarn.

2.5mm / US 1.5 needle for working in the round
Four stitch markers
Tapestry needle

Gauge

32 sts and 44 rows to 10cm / 4" in stocking stitch worked in the round, blocked.

Sizes

0-6m (6-12m, toddler, child) [XS, S, M, L, XL]

Finished circumference (unstretched): 11.5 (13, 14, 15) [16, 17.5, 20, 22.5, 25] cm / 4.5 (5, 5.5, 6) [6.5, 7, 8, 9, 10]"

To fit approx: 12.5 - 14 (14 - 15, 15 - 16, 16 - 17) [18, 19.5, 22, 24,5, 27] cm / 5 – 5.5 (5.5 - 6, 6 - 6.25, 6.25 - 7) [7.25, 7.5, 8.5, 9.5, 10.5]"

Pattern notes

This stitch pattern creates a firmer, textured fabric that is still stretchy. The pattern will work best with a solid, semi-solid or tonally variegated yarn. Highly variegated yarns will mask the textured stitch, but still produce an interesting fabric.

The stitch pattern is given as written and charted instructions.

Pattern

CO 36 (40, 44, 48) [52, 56, 64, 72, 80] sts, PM for start of round and join knitting for working in the round, being careful not to twist.

Cuff

The cuff is worked in 2x2 twisted rib.

Rnd 1: *k2 tbl, p2; repeat from * to end of rnd.
Repeat this rnd until cuff measures 2 (2, 3, 3) [4, 4, 5, 5, 5] cm / 0.75 (0.75, 1.25, 1.25) [1.5, 1.5, 2, 2, 2]" or desired length.

Leg

Knit from either charted or written instructions below.

Written Instructions

Rnds 1 – 4: *p2, k2; rpt from * to end of rnd.
Rnds 5 – 8: *k2, p2; rpt from * to end of rnd.

Work rnd 1 - 8; 1 (1, 2, 2) [4, 5, 5, 6, 6] more times.
Then work rnds 1 - 4 another 0(1, 0, 1) [1, 1, 1, 1, 1] times.

Total rnds 16 (20, 24, 28) [44, 52, 52, 60, 60].

Charted Instructions

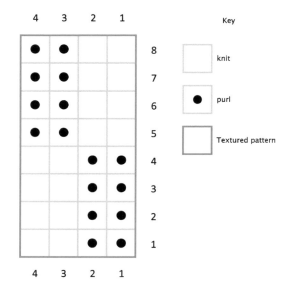

Work rnds 1 - 8; 2 (2, 3, 3) [5, 6, 6, 7, 7] times. Then work rnds 1 - 4 another 0 (1, 0, 1) [1, 1, 1, 1, 1] times.

Total rnds 16 (20, 24, 28) [44, 52, 52, 60, 60].

Heel Flap

Shift start of round as follows. This centres the pattern on the foot.

0-6m and toddler and XS

RM, k2, p1, PM. This is the new start of your round.

All Other Sizes

RM, p1, PM. This is the new start of your round.

The heel is worked, back and forth, over the next 18 (20, 22, 24) [26, 28, 32, 36, 40] sts; leave the other sts unworked.

Follow instructions for your chosen size

0-6m, toddler and XS

Row 1 (RS): sl1, *k2tbl, p2; rpt from * to last st, k1.

Row 2 (WS): sl1, *p2tbl, k2; rpt from * to last st, p1.

All Other Sizes

Row 1 (RS): sl1, *k2tbl, p2; rpt from * to last 3 sts, k2 tbl, p1.
Row 2 (WS): sl1, *p2tbl, k2; rpt from * to last 3 st, p2tbl, k1.

Repeat these 2 rows 6 (7, 8, 9) [10, 11, 12, 13, 14] more times.

Total heel rows 14 (16, 18, 20) [22, 24, 26, 28, 30].

Heel Turn

Row 1: sl1, k10 (12, 12, 14) [14, 16, 18, 20, 22] ssk, k1, turn.
Row 2: sl1, p5 (7, 5, 7) [5, 7, 7, 7, 7] p2tog, p1, turn.

Row 3: sl1, knit to 1 stitch before gap, ssk (stitch before and after gap), k1, turn.
Row 4: sl1, purl to 1 stitch before gap, p2tog (stitch before and after gap), p1, turn.

Repeat rows 3 and 4 until all stitches have been worked.

12 (14, 14, 16) [16, 18, 20, 22, 24) sts remain on needle.

Gusset Set Up

Please read notes about the textured pattern below before starting the next round.

Rnd 1: k6 (7, 7, 8) [8, 9, 10, 11, 12] PM for new start of rnd, k6 (7, 7, 8) [8, 9, 10, 11, 12]. PU and knit 7 (8, 9, 10) [11, 12, 13, 14, 15] sts, M1, PM(A), work across instep in established pattern, starting at rnd 1 (see notes below), PM (B), M1, PU and knit 7 (8, 9, 10) [11, 12, 13, 14, 15] sts, k to end of rnd. 46 (52, 56, 62) [66, 72, 80, 88, 96] sts.

Textured Stitch Pattern Notes

The textured pattern only continues on the top of the foot, the rest of the sock is knitted in stocking stitch. The pattern repeat is slightly different on the top of the foot as it starts and ends with a single stitch.

To help you keep track, I advise placing two stitch markers M(A) and M(B) at either side of the instep 18 (20, 22, 24) [26, 28, 32, 36, 40] sts.

Textured Stitch Pattern for Top of Foot

Written Instructions

Start on rnd 1 for 0-6m and toddler sizes.
Start on rnd 5 for all other sizes.

Rnd 1 – 4: k1, *p2, k2; rpt from * to last st, p1.
Rnd 5 – 8: p1, *k2, p2; rpt from * to last st, k1.

Charted Instructions

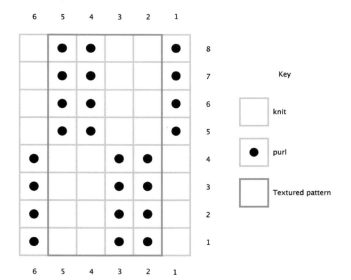

Gusset Decreases

Rnd 1: knit to 2 sts before M(A), k2tog, knit across instep in pattern, SM (B), SSK, knit to end of rnd.

Rnd 2: knit to M(A), knit across instep in pattern to M(B), knit to end of rnd.

Repeat these two rows until you have 36 (40, 44, 48) [52, 56, 64, 72, 80] sts remaining.

Foot

Knit to M(A). This is the start of your new rnd.
Next rnd: Work instep in established pattern to M(B), knit to end of rnd.

Continue working in this way until the foot measures 2 (2, 2.5, 3) [3, 3.5, 4, 5, 5] cm / 0.75 (0.75, 1, 1.25) [1.25, 1.25, 1.5, 2, 2]" less than required foot length. **Remove marker B**

Toe

Shift start of round: RM(A), k3 (3, 4, 4) [4, 4, 5, 6, 6], PM(A). This is the new start of your rnd.

You will now place new markers to keep track of the toe decreases.

Rnd 1: start of rnd M(A) k12 (14, 14, 16) [18, 20, 22, 24, 28], PM(B), k12 (13, 15, 16) [17, 18, 21, 24, 26], PM(C), k12 (13, 15, 16) [17, 18 (21, 24, 26].

Rnd 2: *k1, skpo, knit to 3 before M, k2tog, k1, SM; rpt from * to end of rnd.
Rnd 3: knit.

Repeat rnds 2 and 3 until you have 12 (16, 14, 12) [16, 14, 16, 12, 14) sts rem.

Toddler, S and XL
Next rnd: k1, skpo, k2tog, k1, SM(B), skpo, k2tog, SM(C), skpo, k2tog (8 sts rem)

6-12m, XS and M
Next rnd: k1, skpo, k2tog, k1, SM(B), skpo, k1, k2tog, SM(C), skpo, k1, k2tog (10 sts rem)

0-6, Child and L
Next rnd: *k1, k2tog, k1, SM; rpt from * to end of rnd (9 sts rem)

All sizes

Cut 20cm tail and thread through remaining 9 (10, 8, 9) [10, 8, 10, 9, 8] sts, pull tightly and secure end by weaving in.

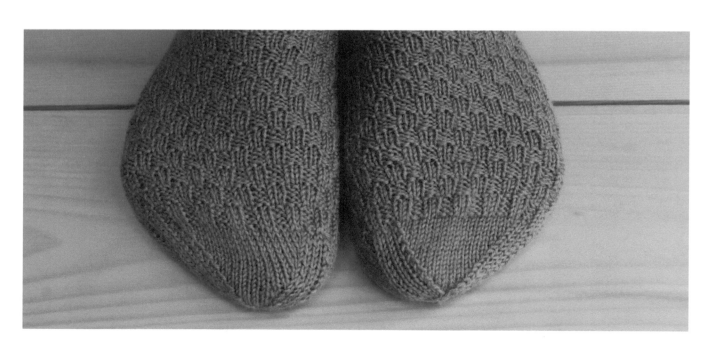

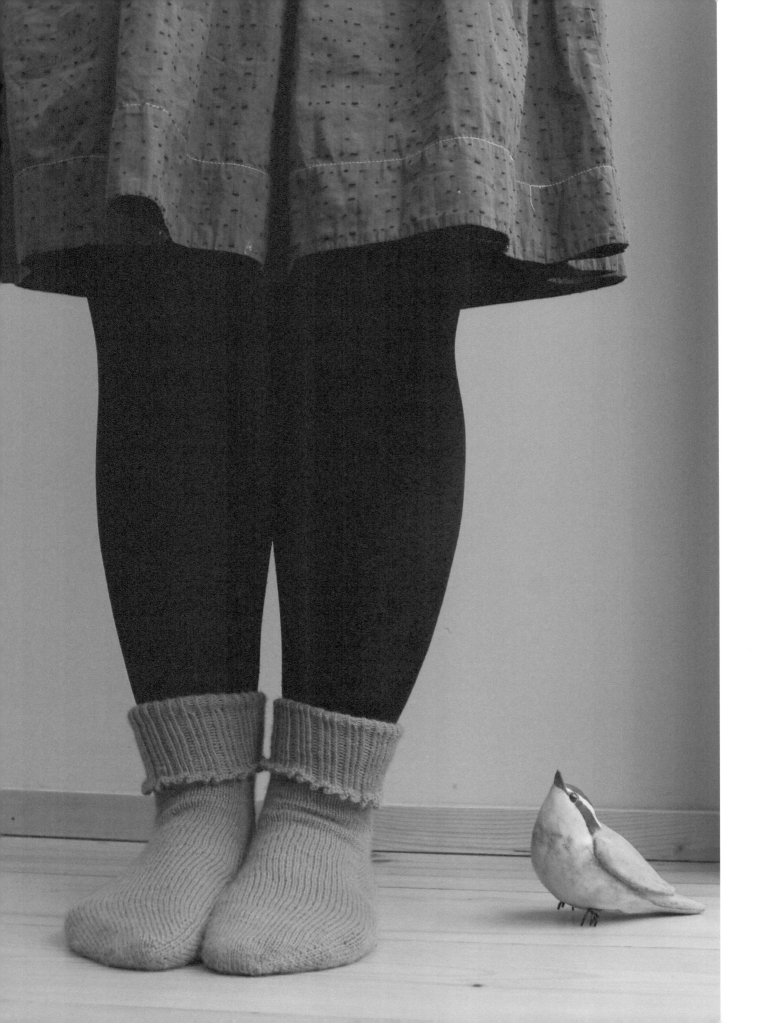

Fabulous toe up socks for everyone: Planum is the perfect choice for all the family. The faux heel flap offers a great fit, especially for those with high insteps, and the clever fold-over ribbed cuff is designed to stay up while looking stylish. Add a feminine finish with a picot edge, or leave the ribbed cuff plain for a practical unisex look.

Materials

West Yorkshire Spinners Signature (4 ply; 75% wool, 25% nylon; 400m/437 yds per 100g ball)
Shade: Pennyroyal; 1 x 100g ball

Yardage per size varies. Baby and toddler (allow 35 – 40g), child (allow 50 – 60g), adult sizes will depend on the size and foot length; allow up to 100g for XS, S and M in a UK size 6. For larger sizes and over a UK size 7 you may need up to 150g of yarn.

2.5mm / US 1.5 needle for working in the round
Four stitch markers
Tapestry needle

Gauge

32 sts and 44 rows to 10cm / 4" in stocking stitch worked in the round, blocked.

Sizes

0-6m (6-12m, toddler, child) [XS, S, M, L, XL]

Finished circumference (unstretched): 11.5 (13, 14, 15) [16, 17.5, 20, 22.5, 25] cm / 4.5 (5, 5.5, 6) [6.5, 7, 8, 9, 10]"

To fit approx: 12.5 - 14 (14 - 15, 15 - 16, 16 - 17) [18, 19.5, 22, 24,5, 27] cm / 5 – 5.5 (5.5 - 6, 6 - 6.25, 6.25 - 7) [7.25, 7.5, 8.5, 9.5, 10.5]"

Pattern notes

The heel length is calculated using the row gauge given in this pattern. If your gauge is different please remember that this will affect the length of the foot.

The four smaller sizes have been adjusted for the flatter foot of babies and younger children. You will notice a fairly big change between the child size and XS, so please bear this in mind when selecting sizes. If you have a child with a high instep they may benefit from the XS size over the child size, providing the general sizing works for them.

Pattern

Toe

Use Judy's Magic Cast On. CO 12 (16, 16, 16) [16, 20, 20, 20, 24] sts.

Place two markers: one to mark start of rnd M(A) and the other to mark your halfway point 6 (8, 8, 8) [8, 10, 10, 10, 12] sts M(B).

The stitches between M(A) and M(B) are your instep stitches, and the stitches between M(B) and then end of the rnd form the gusset stitches.

Rnd 1: *kfb, knit to 2 sts before M(B), kfb, k1; rpt from * to end of rnd.
Repeat rnd 1 (1, 1, 2) [2, 2, 2, 3, 3] times more. 20(24, 24, 28) [28, 32, 32, 36, 40] sts.
Next rnd: Knit.

Next rnd: *kfb, knit to 2 sts before M(B), kfb, k1; rpt from * to end of rnd. 24 (28, 28, 32) [32, 36, 36, 40, 44] sts.
Next rnd: Knit.

Repeat these two rnds 3 (3, 4, 4) [5, 5, 7, 8, 9] more times. 36 (40, 44, 48) [52, 56, 64, 72, 80] sts

Foot

Next rnd: knit.
Repeat this rnd until the foot measures 5 (6, 6.5, 7.5) [9.5, 10.5, 12, 13.5, 15]cm / 2 (2.25, 2.5, 3) [3.75, 4, 4.5, 5.25, 6]" less than the desired total foot length.

Gusset Increases

Maintain M(B) position as set for toe.

Rnd 1: k to M(B), SM, kfb, knit to last 2 sts, kfb, k1.
Rnd 2: knit.

Rpt rnds 1 and 2; 3 (4, 5, 6) [11, 12, 14, 16, 18] more times. Then rpt rnd 1, once more.

Total rnds worked 9 (11, 13, 15) [25, 27, 31, 35, 39].

Place another two markers, C and D, to help you keep track of the short rows for the heel turn. Maintain M(A) as the start of your round.

Next rnd: k18 (20, 22, 24) [26, 28, 32, 36, 40], slip M(B), k5 (6, 7, 8) [13, 14, 16, 18, 20], PM(C), k18 (20, 22, 24) [26, 28, 32, 36, 40], PM(D), k5 (6, 7, 8) [13, 14, 16, 18, 20].

46 (52, 58, 64) [78, 84, 96, 108, 120] sts.

Take time to check your stitch distribution; it is important for the heel turn.

Instep:
Between M(A) start of round and M(B) 18 (20, 22, 24) [26, 28, 32, 36, 40] sts.
Gusset:
Between M(B) and M(C) 5 (6, 7, 8) [13, 14, 16, 18, 20] sts.
Between M(C) and M(D) 18 (20, 22, 24) [26, 28, 32, 36, 40] sts.
Between M(D) and end of round 5 (6, 7, 8) [13, 14, 16, 18, 20] sts.

Heel Turn

Notes on wrap and turn can be found on page 16.

Knit across instep.
The next section is worked back and forth using short rows on the gusset needle only.

Row 1: knit to stitch before M(D), W&T.
Row 2: purl to stitch before M(C), W&T.
Row 3: knit to st before last wrapped stitch, W&T.
Row 4: purl to st before last wrapped stitch, W&T.

Continue working row 3&4 until you have 6 (6, 8, 8) [10, 10, 12, 12, 14] centre stitches with 6 (7, 7, 8) [8, 9, 10, 12, 13] wrapped stitches on either side.

Next rnd (RS): knit to end of heel, working wraps as you come to them; knit across instep: this is now the end of your rnd.

Heel Flap

Row 1: knit to 1 stitch before M(D), working any wraps you come to. SSK, using the two stitches either side of M(D); turn.

Pull your work snug here to avoid baggy decreases.

Row 2: *sl1, p1; rpt from * to two stitches before M(C), sl1, p2tog, using the two stitches either side as before; turn.

Row 3: sl1, knit to one st before the gap, SSK, turn.

Row 4: *sl1, p1; rpt from * to two stitches before the gap, sl1, p2tog, turn.

Repeat rows 3&4 until you have one stitch left on either side of the gusset needle.

Next rnd: sl1, knit to one st before the gap, SSK, do not turn, knit across instep.

Next rnd: M1R, k2tog (using the first two sts of the gusset needle), knit across gusset needle, M1L, knit across instep needle.

Next rnd: k2tog, k16 (18, 20, 22) [24, 26, 30, 34, 38] SSK, k18 (20, 22, 24) [26, 28, 32, 36, 40].

36 (40, 44, 48) [52, 56, 64, 72, 80] sts.

Leg

Next rnd: knit.
Rpt this rnd until leg measures 2 (2, 3, 4) [4, 5, 5, 6, 6]cm / 0.75 (0.75, 1.25, 1.5) [1.5, 2, 2, 2.25, 2.25]" or desired length.

Cuff

Rib Section One
Next rnd: *k1 tbl, p1; rpt from * to end of rnd.
Rpt this rnd until cuff section one measures 2 (2, 3, 3) [4, 5, 5, 5, 5]cm / 0.75 (0.75, 1.25, 1.25) [1.5, 2, 2, 2, 2]" or desired length.

Rib Section Two
Next rnd: *k1, p3; rpt from * to end of rnd.
Rpt this rnd until cuff section two measures 3 (3, 4, 4) [5, 6, 6, 6, 6]cm / 1.25 (1.25, 1.5, 1.5) [2, 2.25, 2.25, 2.25, 2.25] or 1cm / 0.25" longer than section one.

Finishing the Sock

Plain Cuff
Using Elizabeth Zimmerman's sewn bind off, cast off all sts.

Picot Cuff
*Cast on two sts (using the cable cast on method), cast off 4 sts, pass last worked st from RH needle to LH needle; rpt from * to end of rnd. Cut tail and thread it through the last st to secure.

Weave in ends and block lightly.

Sometimes we need a touch of lace to clothe our dancing feet. These pretty lace socks feature simple lace panels framed by garter ridges. Knitted from the toe up, this sock has a short row heel and a folded picot hemmed cuff.

Materials

West Yorkshire Spinners Signature (4 ply; 75% wool, 25% nylon; 400m/437 yds per 100g ball)
Shade: Blackcurrant Bomb; 1 x 100g ball

Yardage per size varies. Baby and toddler (allow 35 – 40g), child (allow 50 – 60g), adult sizes will depend on the size and foot length; allow up to 100g for XS, S and M in a UK size 6. For larger sizes and over a UK size 7 you may need up to 150g of yarn.

2.5mm / US 1.5 needle for working in the round
Four stitch markers
Tapestry needle

Gauge

32 sts and 44 rows to 10cm / 4" in stocking stitch worked in the round, blocked.
30 sts and 44 rows to 10cm / 4" in lace garter pattern worked in the round, blocked.

Sizes

0-6m (6-12m, toddler, child) [XS, S, M, L, XL]

Finished circumference (unstretched): 10.5 (12, 13, 14) [15, 16.5, 19, 21.5, 24] cm / 4.5 (5, 5.5, 6) [6, 6.5, 7.5, 8.5, 9.5]"

To fit approx: 12.5 - 14 (14 - 15, 15 - 16, 16 - 17) [18, 19.5, 22, 24,5, 27] cm / 5 – 5.5 (5.5 - 6, 6 - 6.25, 6.25 - 7) [7.25, 7.5, 8.5, 9.5, 10.5]"

Phalanges

Pattern notes

The lace pattern creates a very stretchy fabric and the sizes have been adjusted accordingly: please bear this in mind when selecting your chosen size. If in doubt choose a smaller size. The picot cuff is sewn which gives the top of the sock the structure needed to stay up. Be careful not to sew too tightly or too loosely when finishing the socks.

When working the lace pattern, be aware you will sometimes have a YO on the end of your needles: be careful not to lose this stitch.

Pattern

Toe

Use Judy's Magic Cast On. CO 12 (12, 16, 16) [16, 20, 20, 20, 24] sts.
Place two markers. One to mark start of rnd M(A) and the other to mark your halfway point 6 (6, 8, 8) [8, 10, 10, 10, 12] sts M(B).
The stitches between M(A) and M(B) are your instep stitches and the stitches between M(B) and the end of the rnd form the sole stitches.

Rnd 1: *kfb, knit to 2 sts before M(B), kfb, k1; rpt from * to end of rnd.
Rnd 2: knit.

Rpt these two rnds 4 (5, 5, 6) [7, 7, 9, 11, 12] more times. 32 (36, 40, 44) [48, 52, 60, 68, 76] sts

Foot

Maintain M(A) and M(B) position. Lace pattern (work from the written or charted instructions)

Written Instructions

Rnd 1 & 3: k1, p14 (16, 18, 20) [22, 24, 28, 32, 36], k1, SM, knit to end of rnd.
Rnd 2 and all even rnds: knit.

Rnds 5 & 9: k1, *YO, k2tog; rpt from * to one st before M, k1, SM, knit to end of rnd.
Rnd 7: k1, *k2tog, YO; rpt from * to one st before M, k1, SM, knit to end of rnd.

Repeat this ten rnd rpt until foot measures 2 (2.5, 3, 3) [3.5, 3.5, 4.5, 5, 6] cm / 0.75 (1, 1.25, 1.25) [1.5, 1.5, 1.75, 2, 2,25]" less than desired total length.

Chart

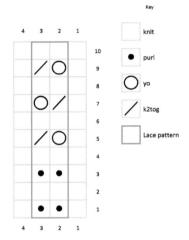

The lace pattern is worked on the top of the foot only. M(B) splits the top and bottom of the foot.

Work from chart, maintaining the knit stitches either side of the lace panel that is repeated 7 (8, 9, 10) [11, 12, 14, 16, 18] times across the top of the foot.

Heel

Work across instep in pattern. Make sure you note which rnd you end on before starting the heel. The heel is worked across the next 16 (18, 20, 22) [24, 26, 30, 34, 38] sts; the other sts remain unworked.

Bottom of Heel

Row 1 (RS): knit to last st, W&T.
Row 2 (WS): purl to last st, W&T.
Row 3: knit to stitch before the first wrapped st you come to, W&T.
Row 4: purl to stitch before the first wrapped st you come to, W&T.

Rpt rows 3 & 4 until 5 (6, 7, 7) [8, 8, 10, 11, 13] sts are wrapped on either side of 6 (6, 6, 8) [8, 10, 10, 12, 12] unwrapped centre sts.

Top of Heel

Row 1 (RS): knit to first wrapped st, work wrap and next st together, W&T next stitch (this is now double wrapped).
Row 2 (WS): sl1, purl to first wrapped st, work wrap and next st together, W&T next stitch (this is now double wrapped).

Rpt rows 1 and 2 until you have one wrapped stitch on either side, ready to work a RS row.

You will now re-join the heel and instep stitches. I have divided this into three steps for clarity. It is worked over one rnd.

Step 1: knit to last st on heel needle, slip this stitch knitwise onto your RH needle, pick up the bar between the heel and instep needle with your RH needle, insert LH needle into 2 sts and k2tog.
Step 2: work across instep stitches in established pattern.
Step 3: pick up bar between instep and heel sts with LH needle. Using RH needle, k2tog with first st of heel. Knit to end of heel. You have now re-joined the heel and instep sts.

Leg

Shift start of rnd: RM, k1, PM. This is the new start of rnd.

Continue working in established pattern using written instructions or chart.

Written Instructions

Rnd 1 & 3: purl.
Rnd 2 and all even rnds: knit.
Rnds 5 and 9: *YO, k2tog; rpt from * to end of rnd.
Rnd 7: *k2tog, YO; rpt from * to end of rnd.

Chart

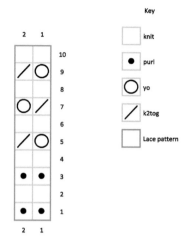

The lace repeat continues around the leg. It is repeated 16 (18, 20, 22) [24, 26, 30, 34, 38] times each rnd.

Repeat this ten rnd rpt until leg measures approximately 2 (2, 3, 4) [4, 4, 5, 5, 5] cm / 0.75 (0.75, 1.25, 1.5) [1.5, 1.5, 2, 2, 2]", or desired length, from heel; ending with rnd 1 or 3.

Cuff

Rnd 1: knit.
Work this rnd 6 (7, 8, 8) [8, 8, 9, 9, 10] more times.
Next rnd: *YO, k2tog; rpt from * to end of rnd.
Rpt rnd 1 another 7 (8, 9, 9) [9, 9, 10, 10, 11) times.

Finishing the Hem

Do not cast off sts. Break yarn, leaving a 30 – 40cm / 12 – 16" long tail.

Carefully fold over hem inwards and sew one live st with each purl bump from the last knit rnd of your lace pattern to secure the hem.

Make sure you secure the hem, but do not sew it too tightly as you will not be able to get the sock over the ankle!

Weave in ends.

Fun ankle socks, perfect for warmer weather. Columns of eyelets and garter stitch create a lovely textured openwork fabric. This sock is knitted from the top down and features a soft and squishy garter stitch short row heel.

Materials

West Yorkshire Spinners Signature (4 ply; 75% wool, 25% nylon; 400m/437 yds per 100g ball)
Shade: Bubblegum; 1 x 100g ball

Yardage per size varies. Baby and toddler (allow 35 – 40g), child (allow 50 – 60g), adult sizes will depend on the size and foot length; allow up to 100g for XS, S and M in a UK size 6. For larger sizes and over a UK size 7 you may need up to 150g of yarn.

2.75mm (US2) needles; for working in the round
2.25mm (US1) needles; for working in the round
Two stitch markers
Tapestry needle

Gauge

36 sts and 44 rows to 10cm / 4" in stocking stitch worked in the round, blocked, using 2.25mm (US1).
28 sts and 44 rows to 10cm / 4" in lace pattern worked in the round, blocked, using 2.25mm (US1).

Sizes

0-6m (6-12m, toddler, child) [XS, S, M, L, XL]

Finished circumference (unstretched): 11.5 (13, 14, 15) [16, 17.5, 20, 22.5, 25] cm / 4.5 (5, 5.5, 6) [6.5, 7, 8, 9, 10]"

To fit approx: 12.5 - 14 (14 - 15, 15 - 16, 16 - 17) [18, 19.5, 22, 24,5, 27] cm / 5 – 5.5 (5.5 - 6, 6 - 6.25, 6.25 - 7) [7.25, 7.5, 8.5, 9.5, 10.5]"

Pattern notes

The lace pattern is very stretchy. I would advise choosing the smaller size if you are unsure of which size to opt for.

The cast on has been adjusted to accommodate the different needle size for the cuff and the loose gauge for the leg. I strongly advise using the first portion of your leg as a swatch. If you are a loose knitter you may need to go down a needle size again for the leg portion.

Pattern

Using 2.75mm / US1.5 needles and German Twisted Cast On, CO 32 (36, 40, 44) [48, 52, 60, 68, 76] sts.

Join to work in the round, taking care not to twist stitches, and PM for start of round.

Cuff

Rnd 1: *k2 tbl, p2; repeat from * to end of rnd.

Repeat this rnd until cuff measures 2 (2, 2.5, 2.5) [4, 4, 4, 4, 4] cm / 0.75 (0.75, 1, 1) [1.5, 1.5, 1.5, 1.5, 1.5]" or desired length.

Leg

Change to 2.25mm (US1) needle.

Rnd 1: *k2tog, YO, k2; rpt from * to end of rnd.
Rnd 2: *K2, p2; rpt from * to end of rnd.

Repeat these two rnds until leg measures 4 (4, 5, 5) [8, 8, 8, 8, 8] cm / 1.5 (1.5, 2, 2) [3.25, 3.25, 3.25, 3.25, 3.25]" or desired length, excluding cuff.

Move BOR one stitch to the right for 0-6m, toddler and XS sizes only.

Heel

The heel is worked using short rows back and forth over the next 16 (18, 20, 22) [24, 26, 30, 34, 38] sts only, in garter stitch (knit every row).

Bottom of heel
Row 1 (RS): knit to last st, W&T.
Row 2 (WS): knit to last st, W&T.
Row 3 (RS): knit to stitch before the first wrapped st you come to, W&T.
Row 4 (WS): knit to stitch before the first wrapped st you come to, W&T.

Rpt rows 3 & 4 until 6 (7, 7, 8) [9, 10, 11, 13, 15] sts are wrapped on either side of 4 (4, 6, 6) [6, 6, 8, 8, 8] unwrapped centre sts.

Top of Heel

With a garter stitch short row heel there is no need to pick up the wraps as they are hidden in the garter stitch.

Row 1: knit to first wrapped st, knit that stitch without picking up the wrap, W&T (you will now have a double wrapped stitch).

Rpt row 1 until you have one wrapped st on either side.

Instep pattern. Start at rnd 1 as written in Foot section below.

Next rnd: knit to last st on heel needle. Slip this stitch knitwise onto your RH needle. PU the bar between the heel and instep needle with your RH needle; insert LH needle into these 2 sts and k2tog.
Work across instep in pattern. (See Foot section below.)
PU bar between instep and heel sts with LH needle; using RH needle, k2tog with first st of heel.

Knit to end of heel.

Foot

The lace pattern is worked on the top of the foot only; the bottom of the foot is worked in stocking stitch. Place M(B) to divide instep and sole stitches. M(A) remains in place as the BOR marker.

The top of the foot is slightly different depending on the size you are working.

0-6m, Toddler and XS

Rnd 1: k1, *k2tog, YO, k2; rpt from * to 3 sts before M(B), k2tog, YO, k1, SM, knit to end of rnd.
Rnd 2: p1, *k2, p2; rpt from * to 3 sts before M(B), k2, p1, SM, knit to end of rnd.

All Other Sizes

Rnd 1: k2, *k2tog, YO, k2; rpt from * to 2 sts before M(B), k2, SM, knit to end of rnd.
Rnd 2: p2, *k2, p2; rpt from * to 2 sts before M(B), p2, SM, knit to end of rnd.

Work until foot measures 2 (2, 2, 3) [3.5, 4, 4.5, 5.5, 6.5]cm / 0.75 (0.75, 0.75, 1) [1.25, 1.5, 1.75, 2.25, 2.5]" less than desired length.

Toe

All sizes

Maintain M(A) and M(B) positions.

Rnd 1: *k1, ssk, knit to 3 sts before M(B), k2tog, k1; rpt from * to end of rnd.
Rnd 2: knit.

Repeat these two rnds 2 (3, 3, 4) [4, 5, 6, 8, 9] more times, ending after a decrease rnd. 20 (20, 24, 24) [28, 28, 32, 32, 36] sts.

Then rpt rnd 1 only, 2(2, 2, 2) [3, 3, 3, 3, 4] times. 12 (12, 16, 16) [16, 16, 20, 20, 20) sts.

Use Kitchener stitch to graft the toe closed.

48

Everybody needs a pair of cabled socks! Here we have columns of mini cables that are the perfect introduction to cable knitting. Knitted from the top down, these socks feature a ribbed heel flap and a V or half-handkerchief heel turn.

Materials

West Yorkshire Spinners Signature (4 ply; 75% wool, 25% nylon; 400m/437 yds per 100g ball)
Shade: Butterscotch; 1 x 100g ball

Yardage per size varies. Baby and toddler (allow 35 – 40g), child (allow 50 – 60g), adult sizes will depend on the size and foot length; allow up to 100g for XS, S and M in a UK size 6. For larger sizes and over a UK size 7 you may need up to 150g of yarn.

2.5mm / US 1.5 needle for working in the round
Three stitch markers
Tapestry needle

Gauge

32 sts and 44 rows to 10cm / 4" in stocking stitch worked in the round, blocked.

36 sts and 44 rows to 10cm / 4" in cable pattern worked in the round, blocked.

Sizes

0-6m (6-12m, toddler, child) [XS, S, M, L, XL]

Finished circumference (unstretched): 11.5 (13, 14, 15) [16, 17.5, 20, 22.5, 25] cm / 4.5 (5, 5.5, 6) [6.5, 7, 8, 9, 10]"

To fit approx: 12.5 - 14 (14 - 15, 15 - 16, 16 - 17) [18, 19.5, 22, 24,5, 27] cm / 5 – 5.5 (5.5 - 6, 6 - 6.25, 6.25 - 7) [7.25, 7.5, 8.5, 9.5, 10.5]"

Pattern notes

The V / half-handkerchief heel turn on these socks is narrow, and creates a fairly pointy heel shape. This works well for babies and smaller children who usually have narrow heels, it is also great for adults with narrower heels. If you have, or are knitting for someone with a broader heel you may find this doesn't offer you the best possible fit.

Pattern

Using 2.5mm / US1.5 needles and German Twisted cast on, CO 36 (40, 44, 48) [54, 58, 66, 74, 82) sts.
Join to work in the round, taking care not to twist stitches, and PM for start of round.

Cuff

Please select the correct set up round for your chosen size.

0-6m, 6-12m, Toddler and Child
Rnd 1: *k1 (1, 1, 2) tbl, p1, k1 (2, 3, 3) tbl, p1, k3 tbl, p1, k2 tbl, p1, k3 tbl, p1, k1 (2, 3, 3) tbl, p1, k1 (1, 1, 2) tbl; repeat from * to end of rnd.

XS
Rnd 1: *k1tbl, p1, k2tbl, [p1, k3tbl, p1, k2tbl] three times, p1, k1tbl; rpt from * to end of rnd.

Small
Rnd 1: *k1tbl, p1, k3tbl, [p1, k3tbl, p1, k2tbl] twice, [p1, k3tbl] twice, p1, k1tbl; rpt from * to end of rnd.

Medium
Rnd 1: *k1tbl, p1, [k2tbl, p1] twice, [k3tbl, p1, k2tbl, p1] three times, k2tbl, p1, k1tbl; rpt from * to end of rnd.

Large
Rnd 1: *k1tbl, [p1, k3tbl] three times, [p1, k2tbl, p1, k3tbl] twice, [p1, k3tbl] twice, p1, k1tbl; rpt from * to end of **rnd.**

X-Large
Rnd 1: *k1tbl, p1, [k2tbl, p1] twice, [k3tbl, p1] twice, [k2tbl, p1, k3tbl, p1] twice, k3tbl, p1, [k2tbl, p1] twice, k1tbl; rpt from * to end of rnd.

Rpt the correct rnd for your size until cuff measures 2 (2, 3, 3) [4, 4, 4, 5, 6, 6) cm / 0.75 (0.75, 1.25, 1.25) [1.5, 1.5, 1.5, 2, 2.25, 2.25)" or desired length.

Leg

Reading from charts or written chart instructions, work rnds 1 – 11 of chart as follows:

0-6m, 6-12m, Toddler and Child

All rnds: *k2 (3, 4, 5), work chart A twice, k2 (3, 4, 5); rpt from * to end of rnd.

0-6m: work rounds 1 – 11 and then rounds 1-9 only.
6-12m: work rnds 1 – 11, twice.
toddler: work rnds 1 – 11, twice, then rnds 1 – 3 once.
child: work rnds 1 – 11 twice, then rounds 1 – 8 once.

XS, S, M, L and XL

All rnds: *k3 (4, 6, 8, 10), work chart A three times, k3 (4, 6, 8, 10); rpt from * to end of rnd.
XS, S, M, L and XL: work rnds 1 – 11 of chart A, three times.

Written Instructions

Rnds 1 - 6: k1, p1, k3, p1, k1.
Round 7: k1, p1, 2/1 LC, p1, k1.
Rnds 8 - 10: k1, p1, k3, p1, k1.
Round 11: k1, p1, 2/1 LC, p1, k1.

Chart

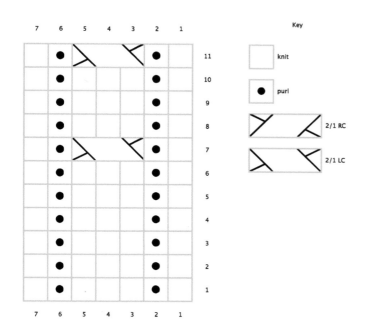

Key

□ knit

● purl

2/1 RC

2/1 LC

Heel Flap

The heel flap is worked over half the total sts. Please work the correct rows for your chosen size.

0-6m, 6-12m, Toddler and Child

Row 1: sl1, k2 (3, 4, 5), p1, k3, p1, k2, p1, k3, p1, k3 (4, 5, 6).
Row 2: sl1, p2 (3, 4, 5), k1, p3, k1, p2, k1, p3, k1, p3 (4, 5, 6).

XS, S, M, L and XL

Row 1 (RS): sl1, k3 (4, 6, 8, 10), [p1, k3, p1, k2] twice, p1, k3, p1, k4 (5, 7, 9, 11).
Row 2 (WS): sl1, p3 (4, 6, 8, 10), [k1, p3, k1, p2] twice, k1, p3, k1, p4 (5, 7, 9, 11).

Repeat these two rows until a total of 12 (14, 16, 18) [20, 22, 24, 26, 28] rows have been worked, ending with a WS row.

Heel Turn

Row 1 (RS): sl1, k8 (10, 10, 12) [13, 15, 17, 19, 21], ssk, k1; turn.

Row 2 (WS): sl1, p1 (3, 1, 3) [2, 4, 4, 4, 4] p2tog, p1; turn.

Row 3 (RS): sl1, knit to 1 st before the gap created on previous row, ssk (to close gap), k1; turn.

Row 4 (WS): sl1, purl to 1 st before the gap created on previous row, p2tog (to close gap), p1; turn.

Repeat rows 3 and 4, working one stitch more each row until you have worked all heel stitches, ending on a WS row. 10 (12, 12, 14) [15, 17, 19, 21, 23] sts rem.

Gusset Set Up

Next round: k5 (6, 6, 7) [8, 8, 9, 10, 11], PM for new start of rnd, k5 (6, 6, 7) [8, 9, 10, 11, 12], PU and knit 6 (7, 8, 9) [10, 11, 12, 13, 14] sts, M1, PM(A), work across instep in established pattern, starting at rnd 1, PM(B), M1, PU and knit 6 (7, 8, 9) [10, 11, 12, 13, 14] sts, k to end of rnd.

42 (48, 42, 58) [64, 70, 78, 86, 94] sts.

Gusset Decreases

Rnd 1: Knit to 2 sts before M(A), k2tog, work across instep in pattern, SM(B), SSK, knit to end of rnd.

Rnd 2: Knit to M(A), work across instep in pattern to M(B), knit to end of rnd.

Repeat these two rows until you have 36 (40, 44, 48) [54, 58, 66, 74, 82] sts rem.

Foot

Next rnd: RM for BOR, knit to M(A): this is now the start of your new rnd.

The top of your foot will be between M(A) and M(B) and is worked in pattern. The sole is worked in stocking stitch.

Work in established pattern until foot measures 3 (3.5, 3.5, 4.5) [5, 5.5, 6.5, 7, 7.5] cm / 1.25 (1.5, 1.5, 1.75) [2, 2.25, 2.5, 2.75, 3]" less than desired length.

The ribbing style pattern continues onto the top of the toe, without the addition of the cable rounds.

Toe

All sizes.

Maintain M(A) and M(B) in position.

The ribbing pattern continues on the top of the foot as set. After each decrease round the edges will be slightly different: just continue to follow the pattern set by the purl stitches.

Rnd 1: k1, ssk, work in established ribbing pattern to 3 sts before M(B), k2tog, k1; SM(B), k1, ssk, knit to last three sts, k2tog, k1.
Rnd 2: work in established ribbing pattern SM(B), knit to end of rnd.

Repeat the last two rounds 5 (6, 6, 7) [9, 10, 12, 13, 15] more times.
12 (12, 16, 16) [18, 18, 18, 22, 22] sts.

Use Kitchener stitch to graft the toe closed.

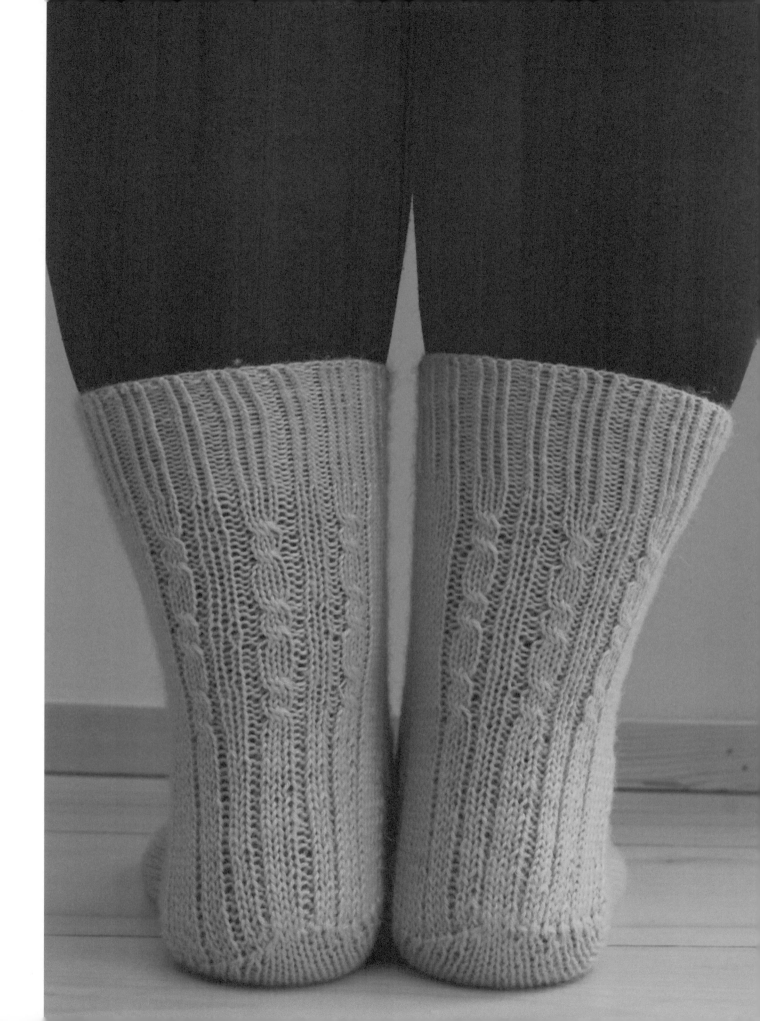

Nothing hugs your feet quite like a pair of ribbed socks. Brevis uses twisted ribbing to give this simple sock a beautifully structured look. The heel is constructed with a heel flap and turned using a German or band heel turn. These are great unisex socks, and perfect for the whole family.

Materials

West Yorkshire Spinners Signature (4 ply; 75% wool, 25% nylon; 400m/437 yds per 100g ball)
Shade: Sour Apple; 1 x 100g ball

Yardage per size varies. Baby and toddler (allow 35 – 40g), child (allow 50 – 60g), adult sizes will depend on the size and foot length; allow up to 100g for XS, S and M in a UK size 6. For larger sizes and over a UK size 7 you may need up to 150g of yarn.

2.5mm (US1.5) needles; for working in the round
Two stitch markers
Tapestry needle

Gauge

32 sts and 44 rows to 10cm / 4" in stocking stitch worked in the round, blocked.

Sizes

0-6m (6-12m, toddler, child) [XS, S, M, L, XL]

Finished circumference (unstretched): 11.5 (13, 14, 15) [16, 17.5, 20, 22.5, 25] cm / 4.5 (5, 5.5, 6) [6.5, 7, 8, 9, 10]"

To fit approx: 12.5 - 14 (14 - 15, 15 - 16, 16 - 17) [18, 19.5, 22, 24,5, 27] cm / 5 – 5.5 (5.5 - 6, 6 - 6.25, 6.25 - 7) [7.25, 7.5, 8.5, 9.5, 10.5]"

Pattern notes

The ribbed sections of this sock are knitted in twisted rib. To create twisted rib, always work the knit stitch through the back loop. Purl stitches are worked as normal.

The twisted rib section continues onto the top of the foot; the sole is worked in stocking stitch.

I would recommend using a very stretchy cast on for this sock to take advantage of the stretchy qualities of the ribbing. My preferred method is the German Twisted Cast On, as it produces a beautiful, stretchy but structured edge.

Pattern

CO 36 (40, 44, 48) [52, 56, 64, 72, 80] sts, PM for start of round and join knitting for working in the round, being careful not to twist.

Leg

NOTE: The leg of this sock is knitted in twisted rib. All knit stitches for the leg are worked through the back loop.

Set up rnd 0-6m, 6-12m, Toddler and Child: *p1, k2 (3, 4, 4) tbl, p1, k2 (2, 2, 3) tbl, p1, k1 tbl, p2, k1 tbl, p1, k2 (2, 2, 3) tbl, p1, k2 (3, 4, 4) tbl, p1; rpt from * to end of rnd.

Set up rnd XS, S, M, L and XL: *p1, k3 (4, 4, 4, 4), p0 (0, 0, 0, 1), k0 (0, 0, 0, 1), p0 (0, 0, 1, 1) k0 (0, 0, 1, 1), p0 (0, 1, 1, 1), k0 (0, 1, 1, 1), p1, k1, p2, k2, p1, k1, p2, k1, p1, k2, p2, k1, p1, k0 (0, 1, 1, 1,) p0 (0, 1, 1, 1), k0 (0, 0, 1, 1), p0 (0, 0, 1, 1), k0 (0, 0, 0, 1) p0 (0, 0, 0, 1), k3 (4, 4, 4, 4), p1; rpt from * to end of rnd.

Repeat this rnd until the leg measures 4 (5, 6.5, 8) [12, 12, 12, 14, 14] cm / 1.5 (2, 2.5, 3.25) [4.75, 4.75, 4.75, 5.5, 5.5]" (or desired leg length).

Heel

The heel is worked in two stages: first the heel flap is knitted and shaped and then the heel is turned.

Once this has been completed, you will pick up stitches along the sides of the heel flap and join the sock in the round again, ready to work the foot.

Heel Flap

Next rnd: Work across the 18 (20, 22, 24) [26, 28, 32, 36, 40] instep stitches in established pattern, set these stitches aside. You are now ready to work the heel flap.

The heel flap is worked back and forth over half the total number of stitches 18 (20, 22, 24) [26, 28, 32, 36, 40].

Row 1: sl1, k17 (19, 21, 23) [25, 27, 31, 35, 39].
Row 2: sl1, p17 (19, 21, 23) [25, 27, 31, 35, 39].

Repeat these two rows 0 (1, 2, 3) [4, 5, 7, 9, 11] more times.
Total rows worked 2 (4, 6, 8) [10, 12, 16, 20, 24].

Shape Heel Flap

Row 1: sl1, k3 (4, 5, 6) [7, 8, 10, 12, 14], k2tog, k6, SSK, k4 (5, 6, 7) [8, 9, 11, 13, 15].
Row 2: sl1, p15 (17, 19, 21) [23, 25, 29, 33, 37].
Row 3: sl1, k2 (3, 4, 5) [6, 7, 9, 11, 13], k2tog, k6, SSK, k3 (4, 5, 6) [7, 8, 10, 12, 14].
Row 4: sl1, p13 (15, 17, 19) [21, 23, 27, 31, 35].
Row 5: sl1, k1 (2, 3, 4) [5, 6, 8, 10, 12], k2tog, k6, SSK, k2 (3, 4, 5) [6, 7, 9, 11, 13].
Row 6: sl1, p11 (13, 15, 17) [19, 21, 25, 29, 33].
Row 7: sl1, k0 (1, 2, 3) [4, 5, 7, 9, 11], k2tog, k6, SSK, k1 (2, 3, 4) [5, 6, 8, 10, 12].
Row 8: sl1, p9 (11, 13, 15) [17, 19, 23, 27, 31].

10 (12, 14, 16) [18, 20, 24, 28, 32] stitches remain.

Heel Turn

All sizes

Row 1: sl1, k7 (8, 9, 10) [11, 12, 14, 16, 18] SSK, turn.
Row 2: sl1, p6, p2tog, turn.

6-12m, Toddler, Child, XS, S, M, L, XL only

Row 3: Sl1, k6, SSK, turn.
Row 4: Sl1, p6, p2tog, turn.

Rpt rows 3 and 4 until 8 sts rem, ending on a WS row.

You will now join the heel to the instep and begin working on the foot.

Next row: Sl1, k7.

Next rnd: PU 5 (6, 7, 8) [9, 10, 12, 14, 16], work instep in established pattern, PU 5 (6, 7, 8) [9, 10, 12, 14, 16]. 36 (40, 44, 48) [52, 56, 64, 72, 80] sts.

Next rnd: k13 (14, 15, 16) [17, 18, 20, 22, 24] PM; this is the now the start of your rnd.

Foot

NOTE: The twisted ribbing continues on the top of the foot only; the sole is knitted in stocking stitch.
Set up rnd 0-6m, 6-12m, toddler and child: *p1, k2 (3, 4, 4) tbl, p1, k2 (2, 2, 3) tbl, p1, k1 tbl, p2, k1 tbl, p1, k2 (2, 2, 3) tbl, p1, k2 (3, 4, 4) tbl, p1, knit to end of rnd.

Set up rnd XS, S, M, L and XL: *p1, k3 (4, 4, 4, 4), p0 (0, 0, 0, 1), k0 (0, 0, 0, 1), p0 (0, 0, 1, 1) k0 (0, 0, 1, 1), p0 (0, 1, 1, 1), k0 (0, 1, 1, 1), p1, k1, p2, k2, p1, k1, p2, k1, p1, k2, p2, k1, p1, k0 (0, 1, 1, 1,) p0 (0, 1, 1, 1), k0 (0, 0, 1, 1), p0 (0, 0, 1, 1), k0 (0, 0, 0, 1) p0 (0, 0, 0, 1), k3 (4, 4, 4, 4), p1, knit to end of rnd.

Work in established pattern until foot measures 2.5 (3, 3.5, 3.5) [4, 4.5, 5, 6, 6.5] cm / 1(1.25, 1.25, 1.25) [1.5, 1.75, 2, 2.25, 2.5]" less than desired length.

Toe

Rnd 1: k18 (20, 22, 24) [26, 28, 32, 36, 40], PM(B), k to end of rnd.

Rnd 2: *k1, ssk, knit to 3 sts before M(B), k2tog, k1; SM(B); rpt from * to end of rnd.
Rnd 3: knit.

Work rnds 2 and 3 until 12 (12, 16, 16) [16, 16, 20, 20, 24] sts remain.

Using Kitchener stitch, graft the toe closed.

Make a statement with the elongated cable of Longus taking centre stage. Knitted from the top down, these socks are slightly longer than the others. They feature a decorative heel flap and the heel is turned using a Dutch or square heel turn.

Materials

West Yorkshire Spinners Signature (4 ply; 75% wool, 25% nylon; 400m/437 yds per 100g ball)
Shade: Poppy Seed; 1 x 100g ball

Yardage per size varies. Baby and toddler (allow 35 – 40g), child (allow 50 – 60g), adult sizes will depend on the size and foot length; allow up to 100g for XS, S and M in a UK size 6. For larger sizes and over a UK size 7 you may need up to 150g of yarn.

2.5mm / US 1.5 needle for working in the round
Three stitch markers
Tapestry needle

Gauge

32 sts and 44 rows to 10cm / 4" in stocking stitch worked in the round, blocked.
36 sts and 44 rows to 10cm / 4" in cable pattern worked in the round, blocked.

Sizes

0-6m (6-12m, toddler, child) [XS, S, M, L, XL]

Finished circumference (unstretched): 11.5 (13, 14, 15) [16, 17.5, 20, 22.5, 25] cm / 4.5 (5, 5.5, 6) [6.5, 7, 8, 9, 10]"

To fit approx: 12.5 - 14 (14 - 15, 15 - 16, 16 - 17) [18, 19.5, 22, 24,5, 27] cm / 5 – 5.5 (5.5 - 6, 6 - 6.25, 6.25 - 7) [7.25, 7.5, 8.5, 9.5, 10.5]"

Pattern notes

The 0-6 and 6-12 month sizes have extra stitches in the leg to accommodate chunky baby ankles. These stitches are decreased for the foot.

Pattern

Using 2.5mm needles and German Twisted Cast On, CO 41 (45, 45, 49) [53, 57, 65, 73, 81] sts.
PM for start of round and join knitting for working in the round, being careful not to twist.

Divide as follows: 21 (23, 23, 25) [27, 29, 33, 37, 41] at front and 20 (22, 22, 24) [26, 28, 32, 36, 40] at back.

I would advise placing a marker to split the front and back (instep and heel) sts.

Cuff

Follow correct set up rnd for size.

0-6m, 6-12m, Toddler and Child
Set up rnd: [k1 tbl, p1] 13 (15, 15, 16) times, p1 (0, 0, 1), k3, p2, k3, p1 (0, 0, 1), [p1, k1 tbl] 2 (3, 3, 3) times, p1.

XS only
Set up rnd: [k1 tbl, p1] 18 times, k3, p2, k3, [p1, k1 tbl] 4 times, p1.

S, M, L and XL
Set up rnd: [k1 tbl, p1] 19 (22, 25, 28) times, PM, p1, k3, p2, k3, p1, PM, [p1, k1 tbl], 4 (5, 6, 7) times, p1..

Work this rnd until cuff measures 2 (2, 2, 2) [4, 4, 5, 5, 5] cm / 0.75 (0.75, 0.75, 0.75) [1.75, 1.75, 2, 2, 2]", or desired length.

Leg

You can choose to work from the written instructions or the chart (see end of pattern) for the cable section.

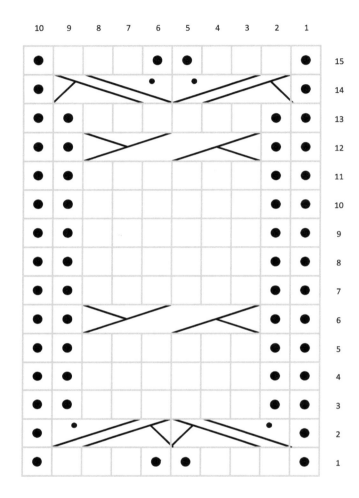

Key

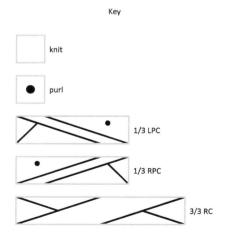

Written Instructions

Rnd 1: p1, k3, p2, k3, p1.
Rnd 2: p1, 1/3 LPC, 1/3 RPC, p1.
Rnd 3 - 5: p2, k6, p2.
Rnd 6: p2, 3/3 RC, p2.
Rnd 7 - 11: p2, k6, p2.
Rnd 12: p2, 3/3 RC, p2.
Rnd 13: p2, k6, p2.
Rnd 14: p1, 1/3 RPC, 1/3 LPC, p1.
Rnd 15: p1, k3, p2, k3, p1.

Start Working Leg Here

All rnds: k26 (29, 29, 32) [35, 38, 44, 50, 56], SM, work Chart A, SM, k5 (6, 6, 7) [8, 9, 11, 13, 15].

Continue working this round while working through Chart A as outlined below.

Work rnd 1 of Chart A 3 (3, 5, 5) [3, 3, 3, 5, 5] times.
Work rnd 2-15 of Chart A.
Work rnd 1 of Chart A 6 (6, 8, 8) [8, 8, 8, 8, 8] times.
Work rnd 2-15 of Chart A.
Work rnd 1 of Chart A 2 (2, 3, 3) [8, 8, 8, 8, 8] times.

Adult S, M, L, XL only

Work rnd 2-15 of Chart A.
Work rnd 1 of Chart A [6, 6, 6, 6, 6] times.

Total rnds worked for leg 39 (39, 44, 44) [67, 67, 67, 69, 69].

Heel

Set up rnd: k21 (23, 23, 25) [27, 29, 33, 37, 41].
You will now work the heel flap over the next 20 (22, 22, 24) [26, 28, 32, 36, 40] sts.

Heel Flap

Row 1(RS): sl1, k4 (5, 5, 6) [7, 8, 10, 12, 14], p1, k3, p2, k3, p1, k5 (6, 6, 7) [8, 9, 11, 13, 15].

Row 2 (WS): sl1, p4 (5, 5, 6) [7, 8, 10, 12, 14], k1, p3, k2, p3, k1, p5 (6, 6, 7) [8, 9, 11, 13, 15].
Rpt these two rows another 6 (7, 7, 8) [9, 10, 12, 13, 14] more times, or until heel flap is desired length.

Total heel flap rows worked 14 (16, 16, 18) [20, 22, 26, 28, 30].

Heel Turn

Row 1(RS): sl1, k12 (13, 13, 15) [16, 17, 20, 23, 25], SSK, turn (make sure you pull your work snug here).
Row 2(WS): sl1, p6 (6, 6, 8) [8, 8, 10, 12, 12], p2tog, turn (make sure you pull your work snug here).
Row 3: sl1, k6 (6, 6, 8) [8, 8, 10, 12, 12], ssk, turn (make sure you pull your work snug here).
Row 4: sl1, p6 (6, 6, 8) [8, 8, 10, 12, 12], p2tog, turn (make sure you pull your work snug here).

Rpt rows 3 & 4 until all stitches have been worked.

8 (8, 8, 10) [10, 10, 12, 14, 14] sts rem.

Gusset

The next round reduces the instep sts and places the markers correctly for neatly decreasing the extra st(s).

0-6m and 6-12 only

Left Sock: k4 (4) PM, k4 (4), PU and knit 7(8), M1, k2, PM(A), k18 (20), PM(B), k1, M1, PU and knit 7(8), k to end of rnd.

Right Sock: k4 (4) PM, k4 (4), PU and knit 7(8), M1, k1, PM(A), k18 (20), PM(B), k2, M1, PU and knit 7(8), k to end of rnd

Toddler – XL

Left Sock: k4 (5) [5, 5, 6, 7, 7] PM, k4 (5) [5, 5, 6, 7, 7], PU and knit 8(9) [10, 11, 13, 14, 15], M1, k1, PM(A), k22 (24) [26, 28, 32, 36, 40], PM(B), M1, PU and knit 8(9) [10, 11, 13, 14, 15], k to end of rnd.

Right Sock: k4 (5) [5, 5, 6, 7, 7] PM, k4 (5) [5, 5, 6, 7, 7], PU and knit 8(9) [10, 11, 13, 14, 15], M1, PM(A), k22 (24) [26, 28, 32, 36, 40], PM(B), k1, M1, PU and knit 8(9) [10, 11, 13, 14, 15], k to end of rnd.

Your stitches will be arranged as follows before you start the gusset decreases.
Instep sts 18 (20, 22, 24) [26, 28, 32, 36, 40]
Total sts 45 (49, 49, 55) [59, 63, 73, 81, 87]

Initial Decrease Rnd

Left Sock
Rnd 1: knit to 3 sts before M(A), k3tog, SM, knit across instep, SM (B), SSK, knit to end of rnd.

Right Sock
Rnd 1: knit to 2 sts before M(A), k2tog, SM, knit across instep to SM (B), SSSK, knit to end of rnd.

Rnd 2: knit.

42 (46, 46, 52) [56, 60, 70, 78, 84] sts rem

Standard Decrease Rnds (Left and Right Socks)

Rnd 3: Knit to 2 sts before M(A), k2tog, knit across instep, SM (B), SSK, knit to end of rnd
Rnd 4: Knit.

Rpt these two rnds 2 (2, 0, 1) [1, 1, 2, 2, 1] more times.

36 (40, 44, 48) [52, 56, 64, 72, 80] sts rem, divided equally for the top of the foot and the sole.
Next rnd: knit to M(A), this is now the new start of rnd

Foot

Next rnd: Knit.

Continue knitting until foot measures 2 (2.5, 3, 3) [3.5, 4, 4.5, 5.5, 6] cm / 0.75 (1, 1.25, 1.25) [1.5, 1.5, 1.75, 2, 2.25]" less than desired length.

Toe

Rnd 1: *k1, ssk, knit to 3 sts before marker, k2tog, k1; SM; rpt from * to end of rnd.
Rnd 2: knit.

Work these two rnds another 4 (5, 6, 6) [7, 8, 9, 11, 12] more times.
Total rnds worked 10 (12, 14, 14) [16, 18, 20, 24, 26]

16 (16, 16, 20) [20, 20, 24, 24, 28] sts rem.

Using Kitchener stitch, graft the toe closed.

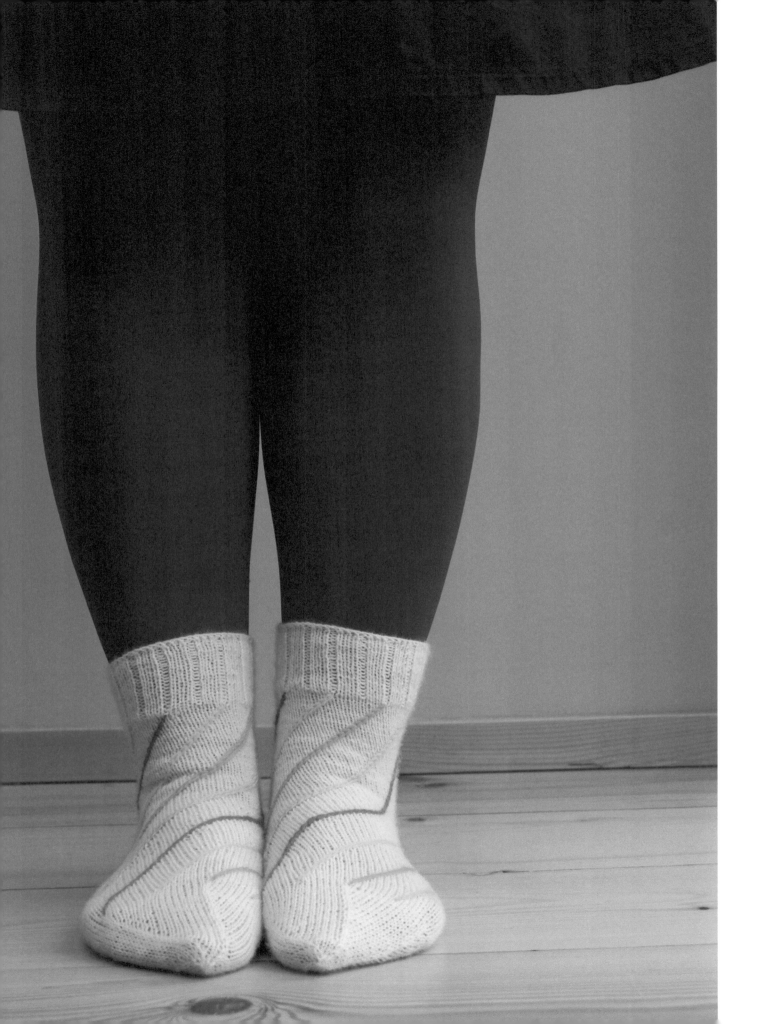

Swirls of colour dance and play around Ossa; the perfect blank canvas for using up sock scraps and celebrating colour. This sock is knitted from the top down and features an afterthought heel. The heel and toe are shaped using swirl decreases, which often look a little unusual but fit beautifully.

Materials

West Yorkshire Spinners Signature (4 ply; 75% wool, 25% nylon; 400m/437 yds per 100g ball)
MC Shade: Milk Bottle; 1 x 100g ball

Yardage per size varies. Baby and toddler (allow 35 – 40g), child (allow 50 – 60g), adult sizes will depend on the size and foot length; allow up to 100g for XS, S and M in a UK size 6. For larger sizes and over a UK size 7 you may need up to 150g of yarn.

CC1: Sour Apple; 5g   CC2: Blackcurrant Bomb; 5g
CC3: Butterscotch; 5g   CC4: Bubblegum; 5g

See pattern notes for additional details on choosing contrast colours.

2.5mm / US 1.5 needle for working in the round
Four stitch markers
Tapestry needle

Gauge

32 sts and 44 rows to 10cm / 4" in stocking stitch worked in the round, blocked.

Sizes

0-6m (6-12m, toddler, child) [XS, S, M, L, XL]

Finished circumference (unstretched): 11.5 (13, 14, 15) [16, 17.5, 20, 22.5, 25] cm / 4.5 (5, 5.5, 6) [6.5, 7, 8, 9, 10]"

To fit approx: 12.5 - 14 (14 - 15, 15 - 16, 16 - 17) [18, 19.5, 22, 24,5, 27] cm / 5 – 5.5 (5.5 - 6, 6 - 6.25, 6.25 - 7) [7.25, 7.5, 8.5, 9.5, 10.5]"

66

Pattern notes

These socks have a snug fit due to the nature of the twisted stitches. Be mindful of gauge when creating these stitches. When selecting a size, if in doubt choose a larger size rather than a smaller one.

Choosing Yarn

Depending on the size you are making, you will create 4 (5, 6, 6) [6, 7, 8, 9, 10] contrast colour bands per sock.

These bands are great for using up scraps of yarn as you only need a small amount of each contrast colour. You could also use a variegated or self-striping yarn on a solid background instead of different colours for the stripes.

Working with the contrast colours can become a little bit tangled if you work from larger balls of yarn. Short strands of yarn about 1m in length make it easier to manage the multiple yarn strands. Placing all the coloured strands inside the sock as you knit helps to keep them tidy too. Alternatively you could use the type of bobbins that are typically used for colourwork.

Creating the Stripes

When working the leg you will add yarn for the twisted slipped stitch columns. Once you have completed the set up rnd you will gradually twist the columns around the leg of the sock using a left twist.

The start of your rnd will shift after each twist rnd. The last twist will use the CC and the first MC stitch of the next rnd. I highly recommend using a stitch marker to keep track of the start of your rnd.

There is a detailed photo explanation of this at the end of the pattern.

Pattern

CO 36 (40, 44, 48) [52, 56, 64, 72, 80] sts.
PM for start of round and join knitting for working in the round, being careful not to twist.

Cuff

Rnd 1: *k3, p1; repeat from * to end of rnd.
Repeat this rnd until cuff measures 2 (2, 2.5, 2.5) [4, 4, 5, 5, 5) cm / 0.75 (0.75, 1, 1) [1.5, 1.5, 2, 2, 2]" or desired length.

Leg

Set Up

Follow correct set up round for your chosen size.

0-6m: *k8, KCC; rpt from * to end of rnd.
6-12m: see below
Toddler: *(k6, KCC) twice, k7, KCC; rpt from * to end of rnd.
Child: see below
XS: *(k8, KCC) twice, k7, KCC; rpt from * to end of rnd.

All other sizes: *k7, KCC; rpt from * to end of rnd.

Create Stripes

Rnd 1: *knit to CC, slip CC; rpt from * to end of rnd.
Rnd 2: knit to CC, LT: rpt from * to end of rnd.

Continue working in this way until the leg measures 6 (7, 8, 8) [9, 10, 10, 10, 10] cm / 2.25 (2.75, 3, 3) [3.5, 4, 4, 4, 4]" or desired length, excluding cuff. Remember to move the marker one stitch to the left before completing a left twist round.

Shift start of rnd to rearrange colour bands.

This ensures you have a new stripe starting at the edge of the foot.

Next rnd: RM, k8 (7, 6, 7) [8, 7, 7, 7, 7], PM; this is now the new start of your rnd.

Place waste yarn for heel.

Next rnd: Work across 18 (20, 22, 24) [26, 28, 32, 36, 40] instep stitches in established pattern.
Then, using waste yarn; 18 (20, 22, 24) [26, 28, 32, 36, 40] sts.
Return these sts from RH needle to LH needle.
Using MC knit to end of rnd.

Foot

The twisted slipped stitch columns continue on the top of the foot only; the sole is knitted in stocking stitch.

Maintain the marker position for BOR and place a second marker to split the instep and the sole stitches. This is important, as it will help you keep track of the shifting colour bands as they move across the foot.

Continue in pattern as set, adding new CC bands as needed to continue the striping pattern across the top of the foot. Maintain the original distance between CC as set for the leg (see set-up round).

Work until distance from waste yarn placed for the heel measures 6 (7, 8, 9) [10, 11, 13, 15, 16] cm / 2.25 (2.75, 3.25, 3.5) [4, 4.25, 5.25, 6, 6.25]" less than is required for the total foot length.

Toe

The toe is worked in the MC only, in stocking stitch.
Divide the toe into 4 sections as follows.

Set up rnd: *k9 (10, 11, 12) [13, 14, 16, 18, 20], PM; rpt from * to end of rnd.

Rnd 1: *knit to 2 sts before M, k2tog, SM; rpt from * to end of rnd.
Rnd 2: knit.

Repeat these two rnds 6 (7, 8, 9) [10, 11, 13, 15, 17] more times.

8 sts rem.

Break yarn, thread through remaining live stitches, pull to close and weave in ends.

Heel

Carefully unravel the waste yarn, picking up stitches on both sides as you go.
Check you have an equal number of sts on each needle.

36 (40, 44, 48) [52, 56, 64, 72, 80] sts.

To avoid holes on the sides of the heel, pick up 2 stitches at each side gap, 1 stitch at each end of the top and bottom needle. A total of 4 sts added to the heel sts.

40 (44, 48, 52) [56, 60, 68, 76, 84] sts.

The heel is worked in the MC only in stocking stitch.

Divide the heel into 4 sections as follows.

Set up rnd: *k10 (11, 12, 13) [14, 15, 17, 19, 21], PM; rpt from * to end of rnd.

Rnd 1: *knit to 2 sts before M, k2tog, SM; rpt from * to end of rnd.
Rnd 2: knit.

Repeat these two rnds 7 (8, 9, 10) [11, 12, 14, 16, 18] more times.

8 sts rem.

Break yarn, thread through remaining live stitches, pull to close and weave in ends.

Left Twist Tutorial

This is the left twist for the Ossa socks. There are many ways to do a left twist, essentially a 1x1 cable. This is my favourite way of doing this twist and it does not require a cable needle.

On the previous round you should slip all the CC stitches purlwise with the yarn held at the back of your work.

STEP ONE

Knit to contrast colour stitch. Remember that this stitch was slipped on the last round.

STEP TWO

Bring right hand needle around the back of work and between the next two stitches on your left hand needle. Knit the second stitch (MC) through the front loop. **Leave this stitch on the needle.**

STEP THREE

Bring right hand needle around to the front of your work and knit the first stitch (CC) through the back loop.

STEP FOUR

You now have two new stitches on your right hand needle and the two original stitches on your left hand needle.

STEP FIVE

Slip both worked stitches off the left hand needle together.

STEP SIX

Continue to work as per the pattern until you reach your next CC slipped stitch. Repeat the left twist again.

At the end of the round

Step 1: Knit to last stitch of the round (CC).

Step 2: Slip stitch to RH needle, remove marker, and slip stitch back onto LH needle. Be careful not to twist the stitch.

Step 3: Perform left twist using last stitch of round (CC) and first stitch of new round (MC). Replace marker.

You have now moved the start of your round on one stitch.

About West Yorkshire Spinners

The yarn used for the designs in this book is from West Yorkshire Spinners, a British company based in Keighley, West Yorkshire.

The Signature 4ply range is perfect for socks, containing 75% wool and 25% nylon with a generous 400m per ball.

There are three stunning colour ranges:

Sweet Shop; featuring six bold shades as seen in Brevis, Bursa, Ossa, Phalanges and Tertius.
Spice Rack; featuring six gorgeous muted shades as seen in Longus, Planum and Tarsi.
Country Birds; wonderful self patterning yarn perfect for socks like Flexor.

More details can be found on their website www.wyspinners.com

Clare Devine is a writer and designer. Originally from South Africa she has nomadic tendencies and after knitting her way around the UK she is now living just outside Melbourne, Australia. She is passionate about all things fibre related (especially if it's grey), knitting, travel and sunshine in equal measures.

Her love of hand knit socks continues to grow each day and she loves encouraging others to try new sock knitting techniques.

Knit Share Love Designs by Clare Devine

Contact details:

For pattern support, enquiries or comments please write to me at clare@knitsharelove.com

www.knitsharelove.com

Instagram: @knitsharelove
Ravelry ID: claredevine

Join my Ravelry group for news, KALs and general chatter

http://www.ravelry.com/groups/knit-share-love